WEALTH
&
HAPPINESS

Using your Wealth To Create A Better Life

DAVID GELLER

ISBN: 146990750X
ISBN-13: 9781469907505
Library of Congress Control Number: 2012900790

DEDICATION

To Heidi Berger Geller,
My loving wife and partner on life's journey,
And to Rachel and Daniel Geller, my wonderful children,
You are my inspiration and my joy.

CONTENTS

ACKNOWLEDGMENTS

I am a lucky man. I am the son of Andrew and Nancy Geller, who love me, encourage me, and who always have faith in me. I have parents who supported, and never diminished, my dreams. My parents encouraged me to pursue my passions and leave the practice of law, even after graciously funding my college and law school education.

I am lucky I come from a close and supportive extended family. I have many close friendships in which we share each other's triumphs and sorrows. I had the privilege to receive a first-class education at Emory University and the University of Michigan Law School.

I am lucky I was born and raised in America, and am living in the twenty-first century.

I am lucky to have been given the chance and the support to write *Wealth and Happiness*. Without that support, this book would never have been written.

My brother, Matthew Geller, and I have always been close, and for the last twenty-one years we have been partners. My relationship with my brother has been one of the cornerstones of my life. Imagine how fortunate I am to have a brother and a partner who shares with me our common vision that wealth management is about more than money and rates of return. It is about helping our clients use their wealth to build more meaningful and satisfying lives. Thank you, Matt, for supporting me in both creating Guided Wealth Transformation® and in taking the time to write *Wealth and Happiness.*

My sister, Margo Geller, has been my friend and companion in this journey. Margo encouraged me to write a book several years before I took pen to paper. She and I have had so many visits together at the Emory Starbuck's sipping coffee and talking about what makes life worth living and honing my ideas. Margo is a licensed clinical social worker who understands the diverse challenges of being a financial planner to successful families. Margo is an insightful and energetic person, and I am glad that our conversations allowed some of those qualities to rub off on me.

My partners and colleagues at GV Financial Advisors have been with me throughout this journey. My GV colleagues served as the proving ground and occasional test subjects for many of the ideas and exercises offered herein. For every half-baked idea offered in its still embryonic stage, they provided keen insight, invaluable wisdom, and incomparable support, and helped create a more coherent and consistent philosophy and process.

To my many clients who have read or will read this book, I want to express my heartfelt thanks. I have been blessed by my relationships with my clients and I have learned so much from each of them. Whether they were merely humoring me or trusting that my passion had a useful purpose, my clients have allowed me to test these concepts on them and patiently endured the sometimes haphazard evolution of Guided Wealth Transformation® (and, in case any clients may be wondering, yes, GWT® still is and likely will always be evolving. The pursuit of truth and the connection between wealth and happiness is an unending journey of discovery.)

I never forget that without our clients, GV Financial Advisors would simply not exist. Thank you to all of you for entrusting us with your money and your dreams.

Thank you to my readers, those poor souls who read early (and not so early) drafts of the book and gave me invaluable suggestions on how to make it better. Thank you to Jane Adamson, Susan Davis, Cindy Wilson, Matthew Geller, Gary Whitehurst, Rebecca Reeves, Therus Kolff, Ramie Tritt, Kathy Betty, Adam Gaslowitz, Carolyn Rose, Margo Geller, Heidi Geller, Randy Oven, Betty Dworschak, and Akhila Aiyer.

I learned early on that while I am told I have some talent as a wealth manager, my skills as a novelist are less than legendary. Doug Childress took my drafts, breathed life into the characters, and kept the book from becoming an unreadable tome. Doug did great work on short notice and endured the many changes suggested by a legion of willing and thoughtful readers.

I owe a special thanks to John and Rebecca Reeves. When I hit the summer doldrums in 2010, they invited Heidi and I to spend a week with them at their beautiful home in Onset, Massachusetts. John and Rebecca were the perfect hosts. They gave me a quiet place to work in the mornings and gave us some great suggestions on how to spend each afternoon recharging my creative brain. It was really great spending a week with you and Heidi, and I appreciate your tremendous hospitality.

Randy Oven has been my own personal guide over the past seven years. (Yes, this is who Randy in the book is named after.) Thank you for helping me on my own journey. I am sure you will recognize a number of your witticisms scattered throughout the book.

There are always folks who operate in the shadows, unsung heroes without whom this book would not have become a reality. Thank you to Akhila Aiyer, Betty Dworschak, and Deanna Krupa, specialists in marketing, writing, and administration. Thanks for smoothing my public persona, helping me to write beautifully, and making sure I show up on time. Throughout this journey, Deanna juggled my schedule, cajoled my clients, and challenged me when I bit off more than I could chew. Thanks to Jeffrey Fong for cover design and illustrations.

My children, Rachel and Daniel Geller, inspire me and have taught me so much. Thank you both for being such great kids and for forgiving all my imperfections being your dad. I love you both dearly and I wrote this book in part hoping that you would be among the first to take its messages about money and happiness to heart.

Maybe most importantly, thank you to Heidi Geller, my wife and best friend. You have lived with my intense focus (you might say "obsession") on how to help people use their wealth to build more satisfying and happier lives. You faithfully read every word of the fable, and we worked side by side to draft the book's concluding chapter, The Model. My life is richer, in the fullest sense of that word, with you by my side.

If the reaction from some of my clients who read drafts of this book is any indication, I expect many of my clients will imagine that they see themselves as the characters and believe this book is about their own unique journey of self-discovery. While some parts of the fable may resemble events that some of my clients experienced, the story and its characters are decidedly and deliberately fictional. The story line and concepts were chosen because of their near-universal appeal. As every good story that mirrors reality says, "Any resemblance to actual people living or dead is purely coincidental."

I also owe a debt of thanks to some people whom I have never had the privilege of meeting, the academics and researchers whose own books provided much of the groundwork for the Guided Wealth Transformation® process and this book. The authors whose works inspired and helped me model my own ideas can be found in the references section.

– David Geller
Atlanta, Georgia
November 2011

INTRODUCTION

I believe the only true purpose of wealth is to help each of us build a more meaningful and satisfying life. After all, it's undeniably true what they say about money—you can't take it with you and there is no award for who dies with the most.

What naturally follows is that the purpose of wealth management is to help clients use their wealth effectively to build a more meaningful and satisfying life.

I have been in the wealth management world for twenty-five years. For a long time, I thought wealth management was about delivering two core competencies to our clients: outstanding investment management based on the ruthless execution of investment fundamentals and giving our clients the information they needed to make decisions in context. It was about helping them answer questions like the following: How much money do I need to retire? What is the best way to save for my children or grandchildren's education? How can I reduce my capital gain taxes when I sell my business?

Those two core competencies are necessary, even vitally important, but they are not sufficient. Why? Because they don't help people overcome the five barriers that prevent them from using their wealth to build a more meaningful and satisfying life. In many cases, just focusing on investments and contextual advice leaves people wondering why they are not happier even though they have climbed the ladder of financial success.

To use your wealth to build a better life, you must go on a paradigm-shifting journey similar to Joe's journey in this book's fable. Many folks embark on that journey when, like Joe, they are in the middle of a difficult life transition. Those transitional moments may include becoming an empty nester, approaching retirement, the death of a parent, spouse or friend, or the sale of a business. Others embark on this journey when they simply get to the point where they are tired of wishing for a more fulfilling life and want to start moving towards a better future.

My firm created Guided Wealth Transformation® (GWT®) to help people embark on that journey. GWT® is a proprietary process we designed to help individuals understand the five barriers and includes over forty tools, such as the Life Priorities cards, specially designed to help families make incremental progress in using their wealth to build a better life. We understand that Guided Wealth Transformation® alone is not sufficient to help successful families use their wealth to build a better life. It must be combined with outstanding investment and contextual advice. For many of us, however, it is the missing piece of the puzzle we have long been searching for.

I hope you enjoy reading the book and trying some of the exercises provided at the end. I hope it helps you think about your money, wealth, and happiness a little differently. The exercises contained in this book are a part of a series of the GWT® Toolkits. If you would like to get additional exercises and tools, including card sets, you can obtain them on our website, http://www.gvfinancial.com. If you have any questions about the exercises or Guided Wealth Transformation®, you may email us at info@gvfinancial.com.

If you would like to subscribe to our e-newsletter, ***Flourish***, in which we continue the conversation on wealth and happiness, please visit our website at http://www.gvfinancial.com. You may opt out of future emails at any time.

We are continually working to improve Guided Wealth Transformation® and I welcome your comments and suggestions. Please feel free to contact me at David@gvfinancial.com.

STORY

MAY: LIGHTNING STRIKES

"Life isn't about waiting for the storm to pass; it is about learning to dance in the rain."

—Anonymous

The day was absolutely miserable in more ways than one. Joe looked at his watch and realized he was not going to be on time this morning. Atlanta traffic was always bad during rush hour, but with a torrential downpour, cars were stacked up more than usual. Several horns beeped, encouraging the masses to move, but Joe didn't have the will to contribute. He was amazed he had even gotten out of bed.

Joe was on his way to meet his financial advisor for breakfast at a diner in Midtown. Randy was actually much more than just an advisor, as he and Joe had become good friends over the last several years. Once a month, the two met for breakfast to talk about Joe's financial future, but their conversation usually ended up being more about their personal lives. Joe looked forward to their monthly breakfasts, but today he was a bit ambivalent. Given recent life circumstances, he would rather crawl into a hole than engage in conversation.

Joe finally made his way off the freeway exit ramp toward the diner. The one-story building was wedged between a gas station and an express mail business, and had a tiny sign that read "Eunice's Rise and Dine." Despite its unassuming presence, Joe had to circle around back to find a parking spot. He turned off the ignition and took a look up at the sky. Rain was still pouring down with no end in sight, and his problems hadn't evaporated either. With a big sigh, Joe made a dash for the diner's front door.

The bell over the diner's entrance chimed loudly as the door briskly swung open. Recognizing Randy at the far end of the narrow room, Joe made his way past the counter to the corner booth where Randy sat having a cup of coffee. Randy was wearing a white knit shirt with olive pants; Joe immediately recognized his salt-and-pepper hair. Upon seeing Randy, Joe felt all his prior ambivalence fade. He was relieved to have someone with whom he could talk.

"Sorry I'm late, Randy," Joe exhaled as he hung his wet trench coat on a hook and slid onto the red vinyl booth.

"I wondered what happened to you," Randy replied, noticing the dark bags under Joe's eyes. "You look like hell. Are you okay?"

"Not really. My life is falling apart as we speak."

"What do you mean your life is falling apart? Is it really that bad?"

"Oh, it's all of that, trust me! Fran told me last night she wants me to move out. Apparently, she's decided she's had enough of our marriage."

"Are you serious? Did that come out of the blue? I thought you guys had a great marriage."

"So did I, but Fran seems to disagree. She wouldn't listen to anything I had to say. It was like she had made up her damn mind without any chance of reconsideration. I'm still in shock."

The waitress came to refill Randy's cup of coffee and offered Joe a cup as well. The smell of bacon permeated the small restaurant, and its sizzle on the open grill could still be heard above the downpour outside. Joe wiped some rain drops from his forehead and buried his face in his hands for a moment.

"I'm sorry," Randy offered. "After all these years, I've never heard you say anything about troubles at home."

"Yeah, I know," Joe replied.

"Were there any warning signs? Anything?"

"If anything, I thought things had been better. Fran has always complained about me working late and not spending time with the family, but in the last several months, her nagging had stopped. I thought she finally understood the financial pressures I was under, but it seems I was wrong. Now the financial pressures are more overwhelming than they have ever been."

"I know the pressures you face, but which ones are getting to you?"

"They're all getting to me! The money I spend on the kids' school, the mortgage payment, basic living expenses, and then the money we just fritter away on I don't know what...all of it. It takes a lot of cash to maintain our lifestyle. And I haven't even included the money I should be saving for retirement," Joe replied, being more animated than before.

"Hold on," Randy interrupted. "I understand your life is expensive, and I know pressures build up, but don't forget you're a very successful attorney and earn a lot of money. You've always supported your family and you're a great saver."

"Well, probably not for long."

"Why do you say that?"

"On top of Fran wanting me out of the house, Seth made it quite clear last week that I need to pull my weight if I want to keep my same income level at the firm."

"He's managing partner of the law firm now?"

"Yeah, and he runs a pretty tight ship. In this economy, his nickel and diming is worse than usual."

"What can I get you, gentlemen?" the waitress asked politely, pulling a small pencil from behind her ear.

Both men knew the menu by heart, but Randy always enjoyed checking just to see if something new had appeared.

"Nothing for me today," Joe stated without making eye contact.

"I'll have the yogurt and fresh fruit," Randy said as he handed the menu back to her.

Joe took a swig of coffee and looked at the streams of rain running down the now-foggy window. It certainly didn't feel like springtime.

"Getting back to Fran, this all seems really strange," Randy remarked. "Are you sure there has been nothing else?"

"Well, Fran has been a little sad since Marcia went off to college last year," Joe replied. "But Mark is still at home, you know. He'll be a senior next year. I'm not sure that's it."

"Has Fran been acting any differently lately?"

"Well, she started going to a community art class six months ago and joined a women's tennis league."

"That's doesn't sound too bad, huh?"

"Randy, I really just don't know. Fran and I have our arguments over everyday stuff, but we have never had any major blowouts over anything big. I really thought, with these new activities, she was adjusting okay to life after kids."

"What about you? Are you doing anything different?"

"Well, since she hasn't been nagging about work as much, I have probably been putting in a few additional hours at the firm. With Seth sounding the alarm, I can hardly say that wasn't justified."

Randy paused and added cream to his recently refreshed coffee. He had known Joe for a long time, but had never seen him as agitated as he was this morning.

"Why don't you tell me exactly how the conversation with Fran went?"

"Well, Mark was at a friend's house, and I had just finished dinner. I got home late, around nine o'clock, so I heated up a plate that Fran had left me in the microwave. After that, I walked into the den to catch some news. But before I turned on the T.V., Fran told me she needed to talk to me."

"What did she say?"

"It was weird. In a very calm voice, she said she wanted me to move out. I was literally stunned by her words and just sat there not knowing how to respond. She then told me she was unhappy and that she needed some time away from me."

Joe's eyes seemed to well up a bit, and he quickly raised his coffee to his lips to collect himself.

"That's tough," Randy said, sensing Joe's sadness.

"Anyway, I asked her what was wrong, and she just said it was too much to get into. She wanted space and time to figure it out."

"No specifics?"

"Nope, just said she was unhappy and wanted me out."

"How did the conversation end?"

"I got irritated and asked her if she was willing to just throw twenty-two years of marriage down the drain. Then she calmly said she just needed time apart. She also said she had not made any final decisions, but she was clear she didn't want me around for a while."

"Wow, not much to go on there."

"I'd say. If she's so damn unhappy, she can move out herself!" Joe said with a rare glimpse of anger.

"I'm really sorry, Joe. I've been there, and I know how hard it is when things are falling apart at home. It just stinks."

"Thanks, Randy. I forget you've been divorced. Maybe it's because it happened before I got to know you so well."

"I haven't forgotten," Randy said with a wan smile. "The things you learn about yourself during a divorce never go away. It's humbling, for sure."

A bowl of vanilla yogurt garnished with blueberries, strawberries, and raspberries landed in front of Randy, and in an almost seamless motion, the waitress refilled both coffee cups with a pot from her right hand. With a toss of a few more creamers, she skirted off to her next customer.

"You sure you're not hungry?" Randy asked.

"I'm sure," Joe replied.

As Randy began to eat, he recalled the fear and hurt he had experienced not too long ago when his ex-wife had filed for divorce. It had been one of the most painful moments in his life, but, in retrospect, it was also one of the most life-changing. Randy knew Joe had a long journey ahead of him, and it was just beginning. Regardless of whether Joe and Fran reconciled, life had thrown Joe a curve he couldn't ignore. Randy knew from his own experience that where Joe ended up was completely up to Joe.

"Joe, I'm really sorry all of this is happening to you. You know I'm happy to help you or Fran any way I can. Obviously, you've got more on your plate than just this. What's happening at work with Seth as the new managing partner?" Randy asked, hoping to shift Joe's focus for a moment.

"Unfortunately, things are nasty there, too," Joe replied. "Seth is insisting that all the partners of the firm either pull their weight or face the consequences."

"Consequences? Sounds ominous."

"Seth is a pretty ominous guy. If I don't hit my figures for the year, next year my salary will be cut back…possibly a lot."

"I don't get it. You've been with the firm for twenty-five years. What about loyalty and tenure? Is anyone else upset at work?"

"Definitely. With the housing collapse and this recession, the guys in real estate and corporate law have really taken a beating, so I'm certainly not alone."

"What's been their response?"

"The bottom line is money talks. Because our salaries are based on our rain-making, all of us are competing against each other for a larger piece of the pie."

"That doesn't leave much room for a cooperative solution."

"Hardly, and Seth is not one for excuses. He won't hear any talk about how bad the economy is or how much other firms are struggling."

"Really? Why not?"

"In his opinion, there is always legal business to be had in any economy. As partners, it's our responsibility to go out and find it."

The sudden crack of thunder outside placed a natural emphasis on Joe's statement. As the rain then increased, Randy lifted the napkin from his lap, wiped a smidgen of yogurt from his chin, and then pushed his bowl to the side.

"I'm always amazed at this John Wayne mentality among attorneys," Randy said. "They think everything is so controllable."

"Well, in Seth's defense, he has been forced to make some tough decisions lately."

"Like what?"

"He met with the executive board and made some expense cuts a few months back; he let several paralegals and junior attorneys go."

"I'm sure that wasn't easy. So are you saying pay cuts for the partners are the last option?"

"I don't know. I just know Seth came into my office yesterday and began his little speech with how thankful he has been for my contributions over the past twenty-five years. I knew what came next wasn't going to be good."

"Kinda putting down some padding before the fall," Randy said, nodding.

"Exactly. Anyway, Seth said he noticed my revenues had dropped over the last few years and told me that unless I got them back up, he would have to cut my salary."

"Was he apologetic at all?"

"As much as he could be. I realize he has a business to run and that means making some hard choices sometimes."

Joe looked down at his watch as the waitress exchanged Randy's empty bowl for the bill.

"I'll take care of that whenever you want," she said, adding some hot coffee to both their cups. Joe reached for the check, but Randy smoothly beat him to it.

"Considering what you've been through this week, breakfast is on me today."

"Thanks, Randy. I'm just at a loss. Almost overnight, everything has begun to crumble. How could I have let this happen?"

"What did you do?!"

"Nothing, but I guess I should have seen both of them coming."

"Joe, I'm sure there were signs along the way, but there's no reason to beat yourself up. You're a good person and have done your best to provide for your family; and on top of that, you've busted your ass at work. You did what you thought was right at the time."

"Yeah, but I guess my best wasn't good enough."

"You've done nothing to intentionally hurt anyone," Randy stated. "You have done all you can to make a good living and be there for your family. Give yourself a break."

"I can't help but feel responsible, Randy."

"I understand, but remember, Joe, self-attack is never a winning strategy. In fact, attacking yourself will only make things worse. Self-compassion is a much better approach."

"I suppose you're right."

"You've been married to Fran a long time, and you've been a top performer for your firm for years. You should be proud of that."

"Uh-huh."

"You shouldn't be so down on yourself. Aren't you a little bit angry with Fran?"

"I'm angry she hit me with this out of the blue without any warning. If there were problems, she should have brought them to my attention."

"Exactly."

"But maybe she did, and I just didn't realize it."

"Marital problems are rarely one-sided. You don't need to shoulder all the blame."

Joe pondered what Randy had said as he took a sip of coffee.

"What about Seth? I mean, you've given most of your life to the firm. Aren't you angry at Seth?"

"Angry at Seth? Why? He's just doing his job. In the end, I'm the one that has to bring home the bacon. If you don't perform, you don't get paid. I guess I'm just not as good as I used to be."

"Look, Joe, you're as good if not better than you were during the good times. I just think you've been hit with a one-two punch, and you're pretty down on yourself."

"Why shouldn't I be? My life is falling apart."

"I understand, but I once heard that anger turned inward can contribute to depression. That might be part of your problem."

"What do you mean?"

"You have given your all to the firm for years and, all of a sudden, your firm is ready to turn its back on you because of factors beyond your control? For most people, that would trigger some anger and frustration."

"Yeah, so?"

"Well because you have justified Seth's actions, you have nowhere else to point that anger except at yourself. Maybe you are angry with yourself for not producing, and now maybe you are feeling depressed and certainly your confidence has been shaken."

"So, are you my shrink now? I thought you were my financial advisor."

"You're right," Randy said, turning his palms upward in supplication. "I am your friend and financial advisor, not your shrink. Speaking as your friend, I just think your depressed mood might be preventing you from thinking clearly. And, to be honest, you have every reason to be depressed over this situation."

"I wouldn't argue with that."

Joe sipped his coffee then slowly shifted his attention from Randy to the window. The rain outside had slowed to a slight sprinkle, and the skies appeared a little brighter than before. A group of women dressed in tennis outfits walked in and sat at a booth at the other end of the diner, and Randy couldn't help but notice Joe glancing their way.

"Are you listening to what I am saying?" Randy asked jolting Joe from his thoughts.

"What? Oh, yeah, I'm listening," Joe replied.

"What's got your attention over there?" Randy asked as he turned to look at the other booth. "I see. Joe, we've been friends for a while. Can I ask you a personal question?"

"Why not? I think we've gotten pretty personal already."

"Have you been faithful to Fran? I mean if that's none of my business, just say so. It's just that her leaving so abruptly is strange."

"The only affair I had while married to Fran has been with the office," Joe replied. "I wasn't checking out the women over there. I noticed they had on tennis outfits and that made me wonder what Fran was doing right now. I realized I haven't wondered about that in a while."

Joe took a sip of coffee. His eyes were swollen and a little red, and Randy again noticed the bags under his eyes. Joe was contemplating Randy's last question.

"Do you think Fran could be having an affair?" Joe asked.

"I wouldn't know, Joe. I don't think you have a lot of facts right now, and things so far just don't make much sense. There's probably a lot more that needs to be said between you two."

"Randy, what is this gonna mean financially for me?"

"I'm confident you are going to be fine financially. You have a solid plan. What kind of pay cut would you be looking at?"

"According to Seth, ten percent…maybe twenty. At first, I felt pretty comfortable with a pay cut because I assumed Fran and I would be able to manage through, but now that I'm looking at a possible divorce, any pay cut could be devastating."

"Don't get too far ahead of yourself, Joe. Try to take things one day at a time. I know you're scared, but working yourself into a panic isn't going to help. You're smart, resilient, talented, and persistent. You can't predict what will happen at work or at home, but I know you'll be okay."

"But if it happens, will I have enough for the kids' colleges and to retire as planned?"

"I don't have your information with me. The truth is that none of us knows what the future holds. I cannot answer those questions, and no one else could either. But you have a great financial base. You need to just take it one day at a time. I'd be happy to run some projections if it would help you feel better."

Joe set his empty coffee mug down and rubbed his face, as if washing it clean, then turned to look outside.

"Look, Joe, you've had a week from hell. And things will probably get worse before they get better. So you just have to take everything step by step."

"I feel as if the rug has been pulled from under me. Despite all I have worked for, everything is just crashing."

"I know it feels that way. We all have this amazing ability to imagine negative outcomes, but, remember, positive outcomes may be just as likely. Everything *might* crash, or it might *not*. You and Fran might work out your differences, and you might land a big client next week."

"But what if that doesn't happen? What if I take a twenty-percent cut in pay and have to survive a divorce? What then?"

"One step at a time, Joe."

"I don't want to be poor after having worked hard all my life. I watched my grandparents worry over every penny they spent. I don't want that life. I've worked too hard."

"Even if all of that comes to pass, I am confident you will be all right. Focus on those things that are most important to you. Focus on your marriage and your family."

Joe wanted to be reassured, but deep down he felt insecure. He thought about Fran. He thought about his children, Marcia and Mark. He thought about his responsibilities. Lost in his thoughts, he didn't even notice that the rain outside had finally stopped.

"I wish I shared your confidence, Randy."

"You don't have to believe it right now, but trust me when I tell you that struggles often give us new perspectives. You'll figure out how to get through this."

Joe stood and grabbed his trench coat and began to put it on. It was completely dry now.

"I need to get going, Randy. Thanks for lending your ear, and for your advice."

"Joe, you are smart, hardworking, and resilient. You're going to be fine. But if you need anything, please give me a call. You'd be giving me the opportunity to help a friend."

"Thank you. I really appreciate it."

"Are we on for next month?"

"Absolutely." On this one question, at least, Joe felt completely confident.

As Joe walked out, the small bell above the door frame echoed throughout the now-empty diner. Randy stood and began donning his own coat, noticing he was the only person left in the restaurant. He nodded thanks to the waitress, who was now enjoying her own well-deserved cup of coffee.

"Come again," she said in a pleasant voice. "And stay out of the rain."

JUNE: A MATTER
OF PERSPECTIVE

No matter what the future holds, there will almost certainly be benefits to the outcome.

As one chapter of our lives closes, it inevitably frees up resources to pursue other opportunities. Nothing is all good or all bad.

The warm summer sun beamed brightly across the small downtown diner as Joe sat alone waiting for Randy. The two overhead fans circulated a mild breeze scented with bacon and eggs. Joe rubbed his hands across the day-old stubble on his face as if to wake himself while waiting for a cup of coffee. If only such a simple gesture could wake him from the nightmare in which he now found himself.

The tiny bell over the diner door rang as Randy arrived right on time. He glanced up and down the diner, examining each of the individual booths, until he saw Joe seated near the back. At first, he almost looked past him. Joe, who was normally meticulously dressed, was wearing an old blue t-shirt and jeans. He looked as if it had been a few days since he had shaved.

"I almost didn't recognize you, Joe," Randy commented as he took a seat on the bench across from Joe. "Good morning," he said tentatively.

"Morning, Randy," Joe replied somewhat sullenly.

"How are you doing?"

"How do you think?"

"By the looks of things, I would say you've been better."

"That would be a fair assessment."

"How are things with Fran?"

"Well, I'm not sure how to answer that exactly. There's certainly been progress, but I'm just not sure it has been in the right direction."

"That doesn't sound good."

"After we spoke last month, I took your advice and tried to get Fran to tell me exactly what was going on. She was reluctant at first to even do that, but eventually I got out of her that she just didn't feel connected to me anymore."

"Did she say how long she's felt that way?"

"Not exactly, but I think it has been happening for years. I told her we needed to go to marriage counseling. She didn't want to at first, but she finally agreed if I promised to move out of the house."

"Really? Did you?"

"Not yet. Even though Fran was being pretty insistent on me getting out, I was able to convince her to continue things as they were until we saw how counseling went."

"How's it going so far?"

"Not so well. I don't think we have made any progress. In fact, I would say things might have gotten worse."

"What do you mean?"

"Fran told me she is pretty bitter. After Marcia went off to college, I guess she realized she had given twenty years of her life to the kids and me. And with the kids needing her less and me still being at the office all the time, she started feeling alone and empty."

"That's not too uncommon, I'm afraid."

"I guess not, but in all of this, Fran said she realized that she and I have nothing in common anymore."

"You've got the kids."

"Well, yeah, but I don't think that's enough for her anymore. Fran said we've grown too far apart and that she just doesn't want to be married to me anymore."

Randy could see Joe's eyes swell as the words left his lips. Joe quickly tried to mask his sadness by taking a swig of his coffee and pretending that the sunshine peeking through the blinds were bothering his eyes.

"Joe, did the marriage counselor help at all? I mean did he or she try to show Fran that your marriage is worth saving?" Randy asked.

"She tried. But Fran's mind seems already made up."

"It just seems strange to have happened so suddenly, Joe. It's not the first time a husband and wife have struggled when their kids leave the nest."

"Yeah, I know," Joe replied. "But, according to Fran, it hasn't been that sudden. She says I have been AWOL for years."

Joe paused as the waitress appeared at the end of their booth.

"What can I get you gentlemen this morning?" she asked with a pleasant smile.

"I'll definitely have a coffee," Randy said. "And how about a bowl of oatmeal with brown sugar and raisins?"

"All right. How about you?" she asked, turning to Joe.

"Umm. I'll have the special. Sunny side up with bacon," Joe replied.

"Sounds good. I'll be right back with your coffee."

Both men sat in silence for a moment. The dark bags under Joe's eyes framed the concern in his eyes. Randy had been where Joe was now not that long ago. He could hardly believe it had been almost six years since his own wife had announced she wanted a divorce. The sting of the memory brought back a flood of emotions. Even though Randy had moved on and was happily remarried, he could easily recall his struggles.

"So you don't have a lot of faith in counseling, huh?" Randy said.

"Not so far. It takes two, and Fran hasn't shown any desire to repair our marriage," Joe replied.

"So, what's next?"

"Hell, I don't know, Randy. I thought you had the crystal ball. All I know is I might be moving out soon if therapy doesn't show any progress in the next couple of weeks. I can see it now…me living in some apartment with rented furniture, eating greasy take-out. That's not where I was supposed to be at this point of my life."

"Sometimes life has a different plan, Joe."

"That doesn't sound too reassuring, especially coming from the guy who helps me with my investment strategies."

"Well, I know it's not what you want to hear right now, but this could be an opportunity for you, Joe."

"An opportunity? It feels more like a major set-back to me! You have a unique way of looking at things, Randy," Joe replied dismissively.

"That's what I hear," Randy said with a grin. "All I mean is that now might be a good time to figure out what is important to you. You know, reevaluate what makes you happy."

Joe was left with that thought as a cup of coffee was placed in front of Randy along with a small bowl of individual creamers.

"Sugar and sweeteners are next to the napkins," the waitress recited. "Your breakfast will be right out."

As fast as she had appeared, the waitress disappeared, leaving Randy to fix his coffee. The diner was a bit warm even this early, but the summer heat never stopped Randy from enjoying his first coffee of the morning.

"So what's with the casual attire, Joe?" Randy asked.

"Huh? Oh, I just didn't get out of bed in time to get ready for the office. I'll get cleaned up after breakfast," Joe replied.

"Oh," Randy said, realizing that in all the time he had known Joe, he had always seen him dressed in a business suit. "Joe, it's going to be all right," Randy said, leaning toward his friend and lowering his voice. "You're going through a tough time, but you will come out the other side, okay? Remember, I've been there. I understand at least some of what you're feeling."

"I just don't know, Randy. Not only am I struggling with Fran, but I stand to lose one of my biggest clients at work. It doesn't feel like everything is going to be okay."

"You've got a lot going for you, Joe. No matter what happens, you'll figure it out."

"Really? If Fran divorces me, I'm going to be looking at a lot of expenses. And if I lose my biggest client, I'm going to take a whopping financial hit. I feel caught between a rock and a hard place. Do I work harder to keep my client and give up on my marriage, or do I devote time to Fran in hopes she may come around? I can't do both."

"That one I can't answer for you, Joe, but I can tell you that it's difficult to make good decisions when you're not thinking clearly and you're still trying to see things from the same point of view."

"I feel like crap because my world is literally falling apart. My God, what do you expect from me?"

"Joe, I get it," Randy said slowly. "Your life is incredibly tough at the moment. I am not trying to sugar-coat the facts. But unless you look at things from a different perspective, you'll continue to make decisions based on fear and worry. And, in my experience, fear-based decisions aren't usually the best."

"Here you go," the waitress said as she slid Joe's plate in front of him. "One special sunny side up with bacon and one bowl of oatmeal for you. Can I get y'all anything else?"

"No, I think we're good," Randy replied with a smile.

"All right, enjoy."

The two men began to eat, but Randy clearly had the bigger appetite. Joe picked up a piece of bacon, took one obligatory bite, and chewed mechanically while Randy blew gently over a steaming spoonful of oatmeal.

"Look, Randy," Joe said somewhat apologetically, "I'm not into that psycho-babble stuff. I'm a simple guy."

"This isn't about being simple or complex, Joe. This is about normal, human reactions. With all that you've been through lately, I wouldn't expect you to be making any big decisions yet. That's normal—smart, even. But if you want to make good decisions, you need to find a way to see past your anxiety."

"What do you mean?" Joe asked suspiciously.

"All you see right now are worst-case scenarios. These possibilities are only causing you to get even more worked up."

"But they are possible."

"Of course they're possible, Joe, but so are many other good outcomes. By focusing only on the worst possible outcomes, you are adding to your own misery. We create much of our own suffering by the way we think about ourselves and the world around us."

"I don't get it," Joe said with a confused look on his face. "How am I causing my own suffering?"

"You're envisioning all of these catastrophes occurring as a result of what's happening in your life, right?" Randy asked rhetorically. "You're picturing living alone in a crappy apartment, having your income level drop, and losing your biggest client."

"That's very possible, though!" Joe replied defensively.

"I understand, but isn't it also possible that Fran may want to get back together? That your client may decide to stay and you could have a great year at the firm?"

"That's wishful thinking."

"Maybe, but they are also possibilities, even if remote ones."

"All right, I see your point. But how does that make me the cause of my misery?"

Randy pulled out a legal pad and pencil and began drawing a triangle with four horizontal lines.

"Joe, you are climbing the Anxiety of Wealth Pyramid or Anxiety Pyramid, for short. At the base of the pyramid, you imagine a future catastrophe. At the moment, you are imagining multiple catastrophes—Fran filing for divorce, ending up living in a crappy apartment, losing a big client, and your income plummeting."

"On that much we agree."

"When you imagine these catastrophes, you instantly begin to feel fear."

"Yeah," Joe agreed.

"When we feel fear, an interesting thing happens," Randy explained. "Fear sets off the fight-or-flight response that we learned about in high school biology. Blood begins to leave your brain and flows into your arms and legs; your body prepares itself either to hit someone or to run away from danger, neither of which would help you in this situation."

"What are you getting at?"

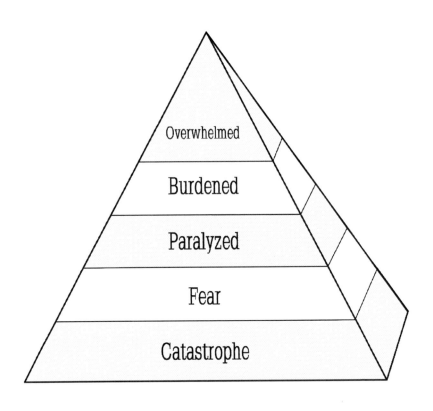

Overwhelmed

Burdened

Paralyzed

Fear

Catastrophe

THE ANXIETY OF WEALTH
PYRAMID

Randy could sense Joe was becoming intrigued and less defensive as his curiosity got the better of him.

"With less blood flowing to your brain, you are less able to make clear decisions. When this happens, your peripheral vision narrows and you literally see fewer options. You end up able to see only negative possibilities and you miss the positive ones. Because your options are limited, you naturally feel the same way."

"Okay," Joe said tentatively.

"When we feel restricted, we also feel burdened. All we see is how unfair life is and how cruel it can be."

Joe stiffened. "Are you implying any of this is somehow fair, Randy?"

"Not at all. This isn't about fairness. It is about you figuring out what to do next. When you are feeling restricted and burdened, it is impossible for you to focus on your real options. Instead, you end up feeling overwhelmed and sorry for yourself. And, as a good lawyer like you knows, that is not a winning strategy."

"So when I envision some bad catastrophe down the road, I naturally feel fear, which causes me to feel more limited?" Joe clarified.

"Exactly, and that leads to a feeling of being burdened. If you have enough of these burdens—as you most certainly do—you can become overwhelmed," Randy explained.

"So if this is a natural, biological response, what's the answer?"

"The key is to get blood back into your brain."

The waitress appeared with a fresh pot of coffee and refreshed Randy's and Joe's cups while placing a few more creamers on the table. Glancing around, she noticed Joe had hardly eaten his breakfast.

"Is your breakfast okay?" she asked, turning to Joe with a look of concern.

"Huh? Oh, it's fine. I'm just not very hungry," Joe replied. "You can take it away."

Randy took advantage of the pause in conversation to take a few bites of his oatmeal, which had finally cooled.

"So how do I get blood back into my brain, Randy?" Joe asked, eager now.

"You have to change your perspective," Randy stated simply. "The first step is to think about what good things have happened to you since we last had breakfast."

"What good things are you talking about? I thought you were listening to me. Now I am beginning to wonder." Joe sat back and crossed his arms over his chest.

"Bear with me, Joe. I know it sounds improbable. Let's just give it a shot. Has anything positive happened to you since our last breakfast?"

"Absolutely not. There's nothing positive about any of this. I really don't want to play this stupid game."

"Hey, you already feel like crap. Why not give it a try?" Randy said softly. "I seriously doubt it will make you feel worse."

"I doubt it will make me feel better."

"Joe, can you just give it a try?" Randy could be as persistent as Joe could be stubborn.

"Okay, it won't make a difference, but I'll play along," Joe said reluctantly.

Randy pushed his oatmeal bowl to the side and prepared to make a list for Joe.

"Okay, so what good things have happened since we last met for breakfast?"

"As I said, nothing." Joe sat stone-faced, conceding nothing, like the good negotiator he was.

"C'mon, Joe. Think about it. Not everything that has happened since then has been bad. You have to see past your big problems and see something positive."

"I can't think of anything."

"Anything at all positive at work? Any good days?"

"Well, I did land a new client a couple of weeks ago. It's this company called Wind Technologies. They design high-efficiency windmills."

"That sounds like a solid client."

"I think so. They want to acquire several key international competitors over the next couple of years, which means a good bit of legal work. They also want me to participate in the negotiation process, which I really enjoy."

"Congratulations, Joe. See? That wasn't so hard. That sounds like a really big positive."

"It is. They could keep me busy with projects for the next couple of years. One acquisition is already in the works."

Randy wrote "new client" on his small white notepad. He couldn't help but notice a bit of animation in Joe's voice when he spoke about Wind Technologies. Joe had been fairly flat during most of breakfast, but that changed when he began describing his new client.

"Okay, what else positive has happened to you lately?" Randy asked.

"Nothing I can think of," Joe answered.

"Boy, you're a tough one. Anything good happen in your family?"

"News flash, Randy. My wife wants me out of the house. What possible good can come of that?"

"How about your kids? Your extended family?"

"Well, I have received a good bit of support from my brother and sister."

"Really?"

"Yeah. It was a coincidence that my brother just happened to call the day after Fran dropped the bomb."

"That was timely."

"I know. To be honest, I'm not really close to either my brother or sister. My brother lives in Charlotte and my sister lives in Seattle. I maybe talk with them a couple of times a year."

"So how did the conversation go?"

"I guess I really needed someone to talk to because I told my brother everything. We were on the phone for nearly an hour. My brother is not an emotional type, but he was surprisingly supportive and gave me some good advice."

"That's really great, Joe."

"Yeah, and I guess he told my sister because she called later that day as well. They both have been really helpful."

"So it's safe to say you have had some pretty positive things happen in the last month."

"Yeah, I guess I have. I didn't really think about them that way because my other problems are so much larger."

"How does that make you feel?"

"I guess a little better."

"Is it safe to say you feel grateful for these things?"

"Yes, I am grateful."

"Is there anything else you are grateful for?"

"I am grateful for my children," Joe offered, no longer feeling combative. "They are both good kids, they are doing well, and I love them dearly."

"Good, that's a start. Maybe a little of the blood is getting back to your brain," Randy said with a smile. "That's the power of gratitude."

"I do have things to be thankful for, I suppose."

The diner had gradually become increasingly crowded. A short line had gathered near the entrance, and the buzz in the small room had become louder. Randy noticed the check lying where his oatmeal bowl had been, and he reached for his wallet as he examined the total.

"So we've covered gratitude, Joe. Now let's talk about faith," Randy said, counting money from his wallet.

"Randy, I told you I'm not a religious kind of guy," Joe replied.

"Faith doesn't always have to be about religion."

"Then what do you mean?"

"Well, what percentage of the time do we face an uncertain future?"

"I don't know. I know I'll be heading to work in a little while. I know what appointments I have scheduled, but I don't know what client will call me with a crisis or will be angry about something. Maybe we can predict the future sixty percent of the time."

"I don't think so. A month ago you probably wouldn't have predicted Fran would want to separate."

"Definitely not. That one blindsided me."

"The truth is we can never predict the future. Although we like to imagine that our lives are safe and predictable, we are constantly on the edge of the unknown. We never know exactly what the next moment will bring."

"Yeah, so?"

"Intuitively, we know this is true, and each of us has come to rely on certain things when life throws us a curve. My question is this: what do you have faith in, or what do you rely on, as you face that uncertain future?"

"I used to rely on my marriage, but not anymore."

"So what do you have faith in now?"

"Well, my brother and sister seem to be people I can rely on. I didn't expect that, but they have been very supportive."

"That's great. What else?"

"I have faith in myself. I know I am a hard worker and I'm incredibly persistent. I believe perseverance and a strong work ethic can overcome a lot of things."

"That's good. There's no question you're a hard worker and very dedicated. That has made you a very successful attorney. So, you have faith in your abilities to succeed come what may, right?"

"I guess so. I mean I know I'm bright, and I know I do a good job for my clients. I listen to them and have close relationships with most of them. I think that's what people want. At least that's what I would want if I were them."

"So you have faith in your family, your work ethic, and your skills as an attorney to help you get through the tough times. Sounds like you have some really good sources of faith, Joe."

"Yeah, I guess I do. You might not believe this coming from me, but I also have faith that all things happen for a reason. I may not be religious, but deep down I do believe this."

"I couldn't agree with you more, Joe. When one door closes, another one opens."

The waitress came and collected the money Randy had left for the check, nodding politely. Joe had been so immersed in the conversation that he hadn't noticed Randy had once again paid for breakfast.

"Randy, I am definitely treating next time. Thanks for getting the tab," Joe said.

"My pleasure, Joe. You didn't even eat anyway."

"Well, I owe you one."

"How do you feel after talking about the things you are grateful for and the things that you put faith in?"

"It's odd, but I do feel better."

"Does that mean you feel a little less burdened and overwhelmed?"

"I guess so. I feel a little more hopeful."

"When you have gratitude and faith, you become less fearful of the future. And with less fear comes a clearer mind."

"Maybe, but I still feel like crap overall. I still see myself coming home to an empty apartment, and Fran still wants a separation. Even if I am thinking more clearly, I still feel pretty bad overall."

"You're going through a really tough time, and you have a long road ahead of you. You're going to feel burdened and overwhelmed at times. That's to be expected. But if you can use this faith and gratitude exercise to reduce your worries, you should be able to think more clearly and make better choices along the way."

"I hear what you're saying, but it still stinks."

"I won't argue with that, Joe. Just hang in there and try to look for the positives."

"All right. Thanks, Randy. Are we on for next month?"

"Definitely."

"I don't want to scare you off with my sob stories. I really appreciate you letting me talk it out, and thanks for the advice. It's really helpful."

"What are friends for? Go on home and get a shower, Joe. Call me if you need anything."

"I will, Randy. Thanks."

The two men rose from their seats as a family of three moved closer to take Randy and Joe's booth. Randy excused himself as Joe made his way to the exit. As he opened the door, the gleaming sun warmed his face. And as he walked around the building to his car, he realized the day did seem a little bit brighter than it had before.

JULY: REASSIGNING PRIORITIES

Unless we remain vigilant, The important things in our life will constantly rob resources from the very important.

Joe made it through the intersection just before the amber light changed color. He was only a few blocks away from Eunice's Rise and Dine. Glancing at the dashboard clock, he realized he was later than he originally thought. "Damn," he muttered under his breath as the next street light was less forgiving than the last. Looking left and then right, Joe thought briefly about running the red light, but thought better of it. He had enough problems already without risking a traffic ticket.

As usual, the diner was packed. A smorgasbord of luxury cars and clunkers peppered the parking lot, highlighting its widespread appeal. Wednesday morning, for some unknown reason, always seemed busier than the other days of the week, and the midsummer heat had certainly not deterred Eunice's faithful. Settling for a spot a block away, Joe walked briskly across the street, carrying his suit jacket in his hand. As he walked in front of the diner, he squinted through the windows to see if Randy was still waiting for him, but the condensation on the inside of the windows made it impossible for him to see in.

Randy was sitting patiently in a booth near the back of the diner, checking email messages on his iPad. Randy's attention was unaffected by the hum of the diner, which provided more of a white-noise background than a distraction. Joe excused himself through the line of patrons still waiting for seats and made his way toward the back of the diner.

"Good morning, Randy," Joe said, tossing his jacket onto the booth. "Late as usual. I'm really sorry."

"I was about to give you a call," Randy replied with a genuine smile. "I was getting a little worried that we had our wires crossed or you were in an accident. Glad you made it."

"Good morning, gentlemen. You'll both be having coffee, as usual?" the waitress asked while wiping off the table.

"That would be great," Joe replied.

"Do you have iced coffee?" Randy asked.

"We do. How would you like it?"

"Cream only," Randy said.

"Actually, make it two," Joe added. "Sounds like just the thing."

"Two iced coffees with cream…be right back."

Joe took a napkin and wiped sweat from his forehead. He glanced around the diner to see if he recognized anyone, but no one looked familiar. He and Randy had been coming to this diner for a few years, but, other than the waitresses, he never saw the same face twice.

"Sorry I was running late again," Joe apologized. "I've been pretty busy and time just got away from me this morning."

"No problem," Randy answered. "I had some emails to respond to while I was waiting. I've been pretty busy myself."

"Oh, yeah? What's happening in your world?"

"I have a longtime client who's selling his business. I'm helping him put together a team of consultants to help him finalize the deal. And there's always stuff going on with the kids."

"Like what?"

"My oldest, Emily, just graduated college, and I'm helping her network for a job. I think she's got a great shot with this reputable PR firm downtown."

"That's great!"

"Yeah, it is. Emily is really smart and hardworking. I'm so proud of her. It would be great if she landed a position here in town."

"Which firm is she interviewing with?"

"She's talked to a few, but the one she's hoping for is Bentley and Crowe."

"That is a great firm. I know a couple of the vice presidents through the office. If you'd like, I could make a few calls."

"That would be great, Joe. I'd really appreciate it."

"No problem. Maybe they could open a few doors for her."

"Two iced coffees," the waitress interrupted, placing cups in front of each of them. "Ready to order?"

"Give us just a second, thanks," Randy replied.

Joe picked up the menu, shifting his attention momentarily to his appetite. His stomach growled almost loud enough for Randy to hear. Joe took a sip of his coffee, hoping to appease the rumblings until he could get some real sustenance.

"What's been going on with you?" Randy asked.

"Too much," Joe replied. "I had a conference call this morning with my new client, Wind Technologies, from London. It started at six-thirty a.m., but it ran a little longer than expected."

"So work has picked up?"

"It's picked up some. I wouldn't say I am slammed, but work, along with everything else I'm dealing with right now, is pretty overwhelming."

"I'm all ears."

"Well, most importantly, Fran and I told the kids what was going on with us."

"Wow. That's a biggie. How did it go?"

"I'm not sure it could have gone well. Marcia came home from college, and so we all sat down as a family. Fran started the conversation. She talked about how she felt increasingly lonely over the last several years and that she and I needed some time apart to figure things out. She said we had grown in different directions."

"What did you say?"

"I told Mark and Marcia we loved them very much and this had nothing to do with them. I told them I didn't really want to separate, but I respected Fran's opinions. Then I told them I had gotten an apartment, not far from the house, where I would be staying."

"You are? What made you decide that?"

"Well, counseling hasn't made much progress and the writing's on the wall. Fran really wants us separated right now. The kids took the news pretty hard."

"What happened?"

"Marcia stood up and yelled at me, saying how it was my fault for working too much and never paying any attention to Fran. She told me I was more concerned about the firm than I was with our family."

"Ouch."

"Mark, on the other hand, just clammed up. He didn't say a word. He just sat there with a stunned look on his face."

"What happened then?"

"Marcia stormed out of the room, ran down the hall, and slammed her bedroom door. I tried to talk to her, but, in between sobs, she kept telling me to just go away."

"And Mark?"

"By the time I had come back from trying to coax Marcia, Mark had gone to his room as well. I knocked on his door, but he just said he didn't want to talk about it."

"I'm really sorry, Joe. You okay?"

"Not really, but it is what it is right now. Marcia's words stung pretty hard, and Mark's withdrawal made me realize how much I want to protect them."

"I understand. But, Joe, you've done your best as a father and have worked hard to provide love and support to your family. Don't lose sight of that."

"Easier said than done. Everything just seems out of whack."

Joe took a sip from his straw and noticed the waitress was headed their way once again. As she walked over, she examined every booth, assessing coffee cups, plates, and bowls as if performing a mental checklist. She seemed to juggle everything so smoothly.

"You gentlemen ready to order?" the waitress asked.

"I'll have a multigrain bagel with light cream cheese and a bowl of your fresh fruit," Randy replied.

"And I'll have a stack of blueberry pancakes with a side of bacon," Joe added.

"Pretty hungry, Joe?"

"I guess so. Since I moved out, my appetite has definitely returned."

"It'll be right out," the waitress said with a smile as she collected both menus.

Randy paused for a moment. He felt his Blackberry vibrate in his pocket and checked the screen to see who was trying to contact him. The screen read "Emily Calling."

Randy excused himself to take the call outside, leaving Joe to enjoy his iced coffee alone for a few moments.

Joe looked around the diner and noticed the mix of people having breakfast. A mom with her two children sat nearby, dressed for a day at the pool. A group of professionals a little farther down was immersed in an intense business conversation. Everyone appeared to have it all under control, going about life as they should. Why did he feel so out of control?

"Sorry about that," Randy said, returning to his seat. "That was Emily. She just had some questions about an application."

"No problem," Joe responded. "It's great she relies on you for guidance. I sure don't feel that way with Marcia these days."

"That will pass in time. What happened after you and Fran had your talk with the kids?"

"I was feeling pretty sorry for myself and headed back to my apartment. But by the time I walked in the door and saw my new life staring back at me, I got pretty pissed. The next thing I knew, I was calling Fran on the phone."

"Uh-oh."

"Uh-oh is right."

"How did that go?"

"Not well. I really let it rip. I told her she was an ungrateful, whining little brat and that she didn't know how good she had it. I told her I had sacrificed everything for the family to make sure the kids were in the best schools and that we had enough to retire on. She has enjoyed a pretty cushy life all because of me."

"Nothing like adding fuel to a fire."

"I dumped a whole can of gas on it, Randy. When I throw a tantrum, I go all out." Joe waved his arms with a levity he did not feel.

"How did Fran react?"

"Like a fire with gas on it. I had to hold the phone away from my ear because she was screaming so loud. She told me how selfish I was and that I only cared about success and money. She said she was done being the only one left to take care of the kids' physical and emotional needs and do all the things it took to keep a family together."

"Sounds to me like you both needed to vent."

"We definitely let it all out. I accused her of living a charmed life with a closet full of clothes and nothing to worry about but getting to spin class on time, and she accused me of being a workaholic obsessed with making money."

"How did the phone call end?"

"She hung up on me."

"I really feel for you, Joe. I know how painful it can be to see your kids hurt, but it adds insult to injury for your kids and your wife to lash out against you. Just remember this is a big shock for everybody, and everyone is going to react in their own way."

The aroma of hot blueberries interrupted their conversation as the waitress delivered Joe's stack of pancakes to the booth along with Randy's bagel and fruit. Reliving the conversation with Fran and the kids had momentarily deterred Joe's appetite. Nonetheless, he methodically began to eat his pancakes. Despite the delicious blend of blueberries and maple syrup, food alone couldn't overcome the anxious knot in his stomach.

"How have things been since the blow-up?" Randy asked after allowing Joe to swallow a few bites of his breakfast.

"Things have calmed down a bit, but Fran and I have had little conversation since," Joe admitted. "Mark still hasn't said much about it to me or Fran, as far as I know. Marcia has always been the more vocal one. I just hate putting my kids under more stress. School is stressful enough."

"It's hard seeing your kids struggle, particularly when you feel responsible. But you shouldn't try to shoulder the entire burden. The truth is you and Fran have grown apart, and both of you share the responsibility."

"I know, but it's still hard."

"You and Fran are not the first couple to have problems, and Marcia and Mark are not the first kids to deal with their parents being separated. Kids are resilient. Mark and Marcia know you love them, and however this turns out, they will be okay."

"I just don't know how everything got so confusing."

Both men paused to take another bite of their breakfast. The mother and her children in the nearby booth were playing a game of "I Spy," targeting items around the diner. Over and over, Joe kept hearing, "I spy with my little eye," reminding him of earlier days when he, Fran, and the kids would travel in the car to Florida. Things seemed so much simpler then…but were they? Maybe it was just his memory looking through rose-colored glasses.

"Joe, do you remember me talking about the five barriers to a meaningful life?" Randy asked, interrupting Joe's trip down memory lane.

"I believe so, but remind me."

"We talked before about having anxiety over money and how faith and gratitude can overcome that barrier. Well, a second barrier is confusion about your life priorities. Things get mixed up, and we often don't spend enough time or attention on what matters most to us."

"Are you saying I'm more at fault because I put work as a priority instead of something else?"

"It's not about assigning blame or deciding who's more at fault, Joe. You and Fran both share in the responsibility for your marriage issues and your children's well-being. You can only control your part."

"So, what's your point?"

"My point is it's a constant challenge to focus our attention on what matters most to us. Often we spend too much time and effort on things that may not be truly important to us."

"But work is important. My career has provided Fran and the kids with opportunities they otherwise wouldn't have had."

"I didn't say work wasn't a priority for you. But where does work rank among all your life priorities? It's easy to distinguish between important and unimportant things in life. The real challenge comes in distinguishing between the important and very important."

"So my focus on work robbed time and energy from other important things?"

"Maybe. That's for you to say. Everyone leads very busy lives these days, and it's common for the important things in our lives to constantly rob resources from those things that are most important to us."

"I think I understand what you're saying."

"Are you willing to play a game?"

"A game? I'm not really in that kind of mood, Randy."

"It'll help you understand what I'm talking about."

"You and your games. All right…shoot."

Randy reached into his bag and pulled out a deck of cards. Pushing their empty plates to the side, he spread the cards before Joe on the table.

"You just happen to carry around a deck of cards?"

"This is no ordinary deck of cards," Randy replied with a grin. "It does have fifty-two cards, but instead of hearts and clubs, each card contains a potential life priority."

"Life priority? Like what?"

"Like luxury lifestyle, being a good parent, having inner peace. Several things."

"So what's the game?"

"I'd like you to go through the cards and sort them into three piles: very important, important, and unimportant priorities."

Randy handed Joe the cards, and Joe diligently began to examine them, tossing cards into one pile or another. As Joe was sorting the cards, Randy pulled a pen from his pocket and wrote "five to fifteen" on a pad of paper.

"Okay, I'm done," Joe said.

"All right, how many cards are in your unimportant pile?"

"Seven," Joe stated after quickly counting them.

"That fits," Randy said with a knowing grin on his face. "Almost everyone puts five to fifteen cards in their unimportant pile. But that means you have a big problem."

"What's that?"

"You've got forty-five cards in your very important and important piles, and it's pretty hard to juggle that many priorities."

"I believe that."

"How many cards are in your very important pile?"

"Let's see…seventeen."

"Okay, out of your very important pile, pick out your ten most important priorities."

"Do I rank them in order?"

"No, life doesn't work that way. At different times, different priorities become more important. If you're worried about losing your job, work might be a top priority. But if you're on vacation, your family might be at the top of the list."

"Okay, so just my top ten."

"Yep."

Randy finished off the last of his iced coffee as Joe took a little more time sorting out the remaining cards. The diner had become less crowded, and the noise level was much more comfortable. Joe continued as the waitress came by and collected their breakfast plates and offered refills on their coffees. Joe was so immersed in the task that he hardly noticed her presence.

"All right, I'm finished," Joe said with satisfaction.

"That took you a little longer, huh?" Randy commented.

"Yeah. Trying to figure out just ten from the pile is tough."

"Exactly. So let's see your top ten."

Joe showed Randy his card selections, which included the following:

- Being a wise and loving parent
- Physical and emotional health
- Having a comfortable life
- Relationship with significant other
- Sex and sexuality
- Financial independence
- Growing and learning
- Connection to siblings
- Close friendships
- Fewer commitments and greater freedom

"All good choices, Joe," Randy said. "Let's go over each one since the cards mean different things to different people. What does being a loving and wise parent mean to you?"

"Well, it means I want to help my children become all they can be. I want them to be happy and I want to have a good relationship with them."

"All right, what about physical and emotional health?"

"That's pretty obvious. I don't want to be sick and want to live a long life."

"That's physical health, but what about emotional health? What does that mean?"

"Hmm. I guess it means I want to be happy."

"Happy is a little vague. What does it take for you to be happy?"

"I'm not sure. I think I'm happy when I am content and truly enjoying all the things in my life."

"For a lot of people, a comfortable life and financial independence are tied together. What do these mean to you?"

"Well, a comfortable life means being able to live in a nice but modest home, buying a decent car every five years or so, being able to travel while staying in pretty nice hotels. I guess it just means being comfortable but not being lavish."

"And financial independence?"

"I guess that's more about retirement and being able to relax. If I am financially independent, I think about not being chained to a job any longer."

"I was surprised to see you had picked relationship with a significant other in your top ten."

"To be honest, so was I. As frustrated and angry as I am with Fran, the bottom line is that I still love her and want to make our marriage work. But I have to face the reality that she doesn't want that anymore."

"That doesn't mean the relationship may not still be important to you. You picked relationships with your siblings and having close friends as well. Sounds like relationships in general might be a high priority."

"I think so. Having my brother, Stewart, and my sister, Sarah, be so supportive of me lately has made me realize how important family is. Plus being alone in my apartment has made it quite clear that I have few close friendships."

"Don't be so sure, Joe. You said you would have never expected Stewart and Sarah to respond like they did, right?"

"That's true. I guess I just don't have anyone I can pick up the phone and invite out for a few beers. I have business clients with whom I'm friendly, and of course you've been great. But it's just not been an area of my life I have focused on in a while."

"Just curious, who would you call if you wanted to connect to a friend?"

"I might call Chris Robbins. He is an old college friend who lives in Atlanta. He sells restaurant equipment. Every time we get together, we always seem to pick right back up where we left off."

"You listed sex and sexuality as well."

"Isn't that pretty self-explanatory?"

"Maybe, but for one person it might mean emotional and physical intimacy while for another it might mean just physical sex."

"Well, for me, sex and sexuality mean being connected to a person physically as well as emotionally. I think intimacy is something couples need to feel connected."

"What about growing and learning?"

"That's one thing I don't think about often enough. One of the best parts of my job is constantly getting new clients who do different things and have different problems. I love learning new things and meeting new challenges."

"Really? Do you have this in your life outside of work?"

"Well, when I travel out of the country, I read about the history of where I am going. I just enjoy learning new things. When I'm learning something new, I'm just naturally happy."

"So that leaves fewer commitments and greater freedom. Isn't that related to not being chained to your job anymore?"

"I suppose it could be, but, for me, fewer commitments and greater freedom is about my life right now. I'm fifty years old and have worked fifty hours a week for more than half my life. I'm tired. All I do is run from the job to my family with no time for me. I want fewer commitments so I can do some of the things I want to do."

"All of that sounds great," Randy summarized. "Now that you've thought about what's most important to you, how do you feel?"

"A little concerned, I guess," Joe replied. "It's pretty clear I have some priorities out of order. I know I have been working too much and neglecting time with my family, but this list of priorities makes me realize I have been neglecting a lot of things."

"It's usually not just one thing."

"Yeah, I suppose so. I guess I just didn't understand how far off track I have become."

"The good news is that with a clear picture of what's important to you, you have the opportunity to get back on track."

"But I can't just change my life overnight. I still have kids, a house, and a job. I still have a bunch of responsibilities."

"Nobody said you had to change everything all at once. Take things one step at a time. Life is about making incremental progress, not immediate perfection."

"I guess I'm just not sure where to start."

"I'll tell you what. Keep the deck of cards and repeat the exercise a few more times to see if your priority choices are consistent. Then you and I can figure out a plan of action."

"A plan of action?"

"Yeah. Decide what small steps you can take to head in the right direction. You might even decide to share your choices with Fran. It might not help your marriage, but it probably won't hurt either."

Joe neatly stacked the deck of cards back together and placed them back in their case. The waitress came by to make sure neither of them wanted anything else before she totaled the bill and placed it on the table. Randy reached for the check, but Joe grabbed it before he had a chance.

"Not today, Randy. I already owe you a couple of breakfasts," Joe said with a rare smile.

"Hey, have it your way," Randy replied, grinning back at Joe.

Joe counted out the proper amount of money for their breakfast and left it on the table next to the check. Replacing his wallet in his back pocket, he picked up the deck of cards along with his jacket.

"Thanks for the cards, Randy," Joe said. "And thanks for the new perspective."

"My pleasure," Randy replied. "Just remember, everything takes time. Be patient with yourself. Changing your perspective on things is a slow process. Just keep moving in the right direction step by step, and, before you know it, you'll be living the life you want to live and seeing things differently."

"Speaking of time, I have to run," Joe said, looking down at his watch. "I have a conference call in twenty minutes."

"No problem. I need to get going as well," Randy replied. "Give me a call if you need anything. Are we on for our regular time next month?"

"Definitely. Thanks for all your help, Randy. You've given me plenty to think about."

"My pleasure. What are friends for?" Randy said, smiling as he stood up to leave.

Randy and Joe walked out together and then parted ways, heading in different directions to their cars. The midsummer heat was already suffocating, and Joe quickly took off the jacket he had only seconds ago put on inside the diner. He thought to himself, *That's a little more comfortable,* and then chuckled to himself, recalling increased comfort as one of his priorities. Taking off his jacket was indeed a very small step in that direction. Surely he could take a little bigger step than that!

AUGUST: REDEFINING WEALTH

"Genuine fearlessness arises with the confidence that we will be able to gather the inner resources necessary to deal with any situation that comes our way."
—Matthieu Ricard

Streaks of purple, orange, and red were layered along the Western sky as the scorching Georgia sun finally made its escape. Dusk had been one of Joe's favorite times of day since he had been a boy, but those days were long past. As he drove just north of Atlanta's beltway, he couldn't recall the last time he had actually taken the time to appreciate the hues and colors of the early evening sky. Life had become too busy. Or maybe, as Randy had suggested, his life priorities had gotten seriously out of whack. As Joe parked his car, he paused to enjoy the beauty of the moment.

Joe was meeting Randy as usual, but the evening was a distinct contrast to the mornings at the diner. The nights alone in his new apartment prompted Joe to invite Randy out for dinner rather than breakfast this month; and as he walked toward the restaurant, he was glad he had company. Mickey's was one of the premier steak places in Atlanta, and Joe couldn't wait to sink his teeth into a juicy steak. As he passed the hostess station, he recognized Randy almost immediately despite the dim lights and dark mahogany tables. Joe looked down at his watch. For once he wasn't late.

"Evenings suit me. I'm on time for a change," Joe said as he sat down in the chair across from Randy.

"I see that," Randy replied with a grin. "How are you, Joe?"

"I'm doing all right. How 'bout you?"

"Couldn't be better. By the way, good call to meet here. I haven't been out for steak in a while, and I always forget about Mickey's."

"Yeah, me, too. It's just a little off the beaten path."

"Laura and I used to eat here a few times a year, but we haven't been in a while."

"How is Laura?"

"Laura's great. We just celebrated our third-year wedding anniversary."

"That's wonderful. I didn't realize it has been that long," Joe remarked.

"Time flies, huh? Yeah, Laura and I just get along so much better than I did with my ex-wife. We're better connected to each other's interests," Randy added.

"I'm sure it's not all peaches and cream."

"We have our disagreements, but we don't ever fight the way I did with my ex. There's just a higher level of respect. We complement each other, make sure there's time for intimacy, and honestly we just have more fun together."

"That sounds really great. I hope I have that again someday."

"You can and you will, Joe."

"I have my doubts about that. I certainly don't see it happening with Fran."

"Why? What's happened lately?"

"It's just that counseling hasn't gone anywhere. I think Fran is just going through the motions to check a box, but ultimately she just wants out. She's already made up her mind."

"I'm sorry to hear that."

A young waiter approached the table and patiently waited a few seconds for Randy and Joe to pause in their conversation. Neatly dressed in a white shirt with black tie, along with a striped bistro apron, he placed a leather-covered menu in front of both of them.

"Gentlemen, may I offer you something to drink?"

"May I see your wine list?" Randy asked.

"Of course," the waiter replied, handing a smaller menu to Randy. "Take a few moments to look it over and I'll be right back," the waiter said, briefly excusing himself.

Randy looked over the list of reds and whites, but then remembered Joe was much more knowledgeable about wines.

"Joe, you're the *connoisseur*," Randy said, passing the wine menu to him. "Would you do the honors?"

"Glad to. Are you in the mood for a red or white?"

"Definitely red. I plan on having steak."

After studying the list briefly, Joe found one that he believed would satisfy their tastes. He placed the menu to the side and took a sip of water while Randy began studying the menu. Despite being a Tuesday evening, Mickey's had attracted a pretty good crowd, and a pleasant buzz of conversation made the restaurant feel alive.

"I know just which steak I'm having," Joe boasted. "I've been thinking about their prime rib all day."

"That's funny, I was thinking the same thing," Randy responded. "Great minds think alike."

"It sure beats frozen dinners in an apartment," Joe commented. "At least every other week Mark stays with me, so I have been cooking some. But my cooking is rusty and it's a far cry from a good steak."

"What else is going on with the kids?"

"That's a bit of a mixed bag," Joe replied, pausing to wet his lips. "Marcia just returned to the University of Michigan. She's accepted things the way they currently are between Fran and me, but I wouldn't say she's happy."

"It takes time. It's a pretty tough pill to swallow."

"I know. Overall, I think she's doing pretty well. Mark, on the other hand, is a different story."

"But he's been the quiet one?"

"On the surface, yes…but deep down he's pretty upset."

"Why? What's going on?"

"Well, for the past month or so, Mark has been staying with me every other week. The apartment is a bit cramped, but we've been making the best of it. When he's there for the week, I try and get home by six-thirty p.m., and, for the most part, I've been able to keep that schedule."

"That doesn't sound bad at all. Sounds like you're getting to spend some one-on-one time together."

"Definitely. But the other night, Mark and his friend had been down the street at a party, and they both got drunk. They walked home from the party, but they were yelling at the top of their lungs. One of the neighbors called the police, and Mark ended up getting arrested for underage drinking and disturbing the peace."

"Mark? That doesn't even sound like him!"

"I know. Mark told the officer to mind his own business, in addition to a few other suggestions. I was expecting him home by eleven, but instead I got a call from the police station."

"Oh, boy. What did Fran say about it?"

"I haven't told her yet. I'm not quite sure how to approach it. I mean, Mark was on my watch when it happened, and it's just going to add more fuel to the fire."

"I would definitely tell Fran sooner rather than later. She'll find out one way or the other anyway."

"I intend to tell her. I'm just dreading it because she'll accuse me of all the same stuff again. You know, how I don't spend enough time with Mark, how I am always at work, *et cetera.*"

"Actually, maybe Mark should be the one who tells her. He is the one who got drunk, not you. How was Mark when you saw him that night?"

"He was sleeping it off when I got down to the police station. I woke him up, and we drove home in silence. We talked about it the next morning."

"What did you say?"

"By then, I wasn't as angry. I told him I knew he was upset about things, but drinking wasn't the answer and only made things worse. I told him I would find an attorney to help, but no matter what happened there was going to be a punishment coming."

"What did he say?"

"He just sat quietly and listened. He did say he was sorry, but he didn't open up much more than that."

The waiter reappeared with a fresh pitcher of ice water, which he used to refresh the glasses on the table.

"Have you gentlemen decided on a wine?" he asked, assuming an upright posture.

"Yes, may we have a bottle of the 1998 Bordeaux?" Joe asked while handing the wine list back to the waiter.

"Of course. As for our specials this evening, gentlemen, we have a double portion veal porterhouse steak served with asparagus sautéed in truffle butter and also a surf and turf special featuring an eight-ounce *filet mignon* topped with grilled lobster with lemon aioli. I'll be back in a moment with your wine."

Joe took another sip of ice water while replaying the scene with Mark over again in his head. Mark had always been well-behaved, polite, and easygoing. But Fran had been concerned about his grades falling over the last few months. Maybe her intuition that Mark was struggling to find his way had been right.

"Joe, do you recall last month when we did the list of priorities?" Randy asked.

"Of course. I pulled out the deck of cards a couple of times since then. Not much to do alone in the apartment, ya know," Joe answered with a wink and a slight smile.

"Did your list stay about the same?"

"Almost identical each time."

"If I remember correctly, one of your priorities was being a wise and loving parent, right?"

"Right."

"So this thing with Mark sounds like a great opportunity for you. How can you line up your life priorities with some actions?"

"I don't know. It seems like I've done enough damage already. I can't help but feel responsible for his struggles. If Fran and I weren't separated, he probably wouldn't be behaving like this."

"You haven't intentionally done anything to Mark. Don't focus on who or what's to blame. Try focusing instead on what you can do to help. Focus on your priorities."

"All right. I'd like to help him resolve his legal issues. I don't want a foolish mistake to be a permanent mark on his record and limit his chances of getting into a good college. I also want to help him deal with any emotions or confusions he's having about Fran and me and just be a resource for him in dealing with the normal teenage stresses."

"Those sounds like reasonable goals. So what's stopping you?"

"I'm not really sure. I guess Mark and I just haven't connected well lately. We haven't been communicating as well recently. I'm not sure where to begin."

"The best way to start is to separate what part of your communication difficulty is a real problem from what part may just be a painful reality."

"I don't understand. What do you mean?"

"Well, a problem is something you can do something about, but a painful reality is something that just is. For example, making time available for Mark is something you can do something about, but forcing Mark to listen or talk to you may just be impossible."

"I see. Well, I am sure I could improve my communication skills. Perhaps that's my biggest problem with Mark right now. I just don't know what to say sometimes."

Both Randy and Joe took a sip of water as they saw the waiter approach with a bottle of red wine, which he neatly opened tableside. Joe examined the label of the Bordeaux and approved his selection with a brief sniff and taste of a sample pour. The waiter poured each man a glass of wine and took their entrée orders before again excusing himself. Joe tasted the wine, which was exquisite. *Randy always seems to know the right things to say*, he thought. Joe wished he had the same talent when it came to Mark.

"I understand that it's Mark's decision whether or not he wants to communicate with me, but I don't know how to improve my ability to talk to him," Joe said, looking down into his wine glass.

"Joe, most of the time, people underestimate their ability to resolve problems," Randy replied reassuringly. "The issue in life is almost never that the problem is too big. Most times, the real issue is that you don't have enough support."

"So how do you get more support?"

"That's easy. You get support by using your wealth."

"I'm already feeling constrained financially. I'm not sure what you mean."

"Think about wealth in broader terms. Money is only one of the six elements of wealth. There are other things that make us wealthy as well."

Randy took out a pad of paper and wrote down the following list of resources:

- Money
- Time
- Talents
- Body and Mind
- Wisdom
- Networks or Community

"These are the six elements of wealth and support available to everyone," Randy said, turning the paper toward Joe so he could see them. "These are your resources to help you overcome any problem."

Joe studied the list while taking a sip of wine. The list seemed pretty straightforward, but exactly how did it apply to his ability to help Mark with his current struggles? And what did this have to do with wealth?

"Randy, I don't mean to be dense, but I'm not sure I understand what these have to do with wealth," Joe humbly admitted.

"Let me ask you a question, Joe," Randy said. "How do you define wealth?"

"Wealth is the amount of financial assets you enjoy."

"That's similar to most people's definition. Most of us equate wealth with money or our net worth. But true wealth is about all the resources you have to help you live the life you desire and to solve your challenges. True wealth consists of six elements. Money is just one of those elements."

"So any one of these six has the ability to make my life wealthier?"

"Exactly!"

Randy excused himself from the table for a moment. As Joe sat alone, he glanced around at the other tables in the restaurant. Some people were casually dressed while others were more formal. On any given day, Joe could have picked the ones he thought were the wealthiest based on their attire, their demeanor, and even the type of cocktail they ordered. But in light of Randy's list, he began to realize his prior assumptions were perhaps incorrect. Just because one has financial wealth doesn't mean one is truly wealthy. It was an obvious truth, perhaps, but one he had neglected to realize.

"Did I miss anything?" Randy said with a smile, returning to his chair.

"Just me trying to figure out how your list solves my problems with Mark," Joe replied with a grin.

"All right, let's start with an easy one. You're an attorney, and Mark is having legal problems. Networking can be a significant resource for support. Who is in your network that can help?"

"I've already called Perry Stevens, who is a good friend of mine, and he's agreed to represent Mark. He thinks he might be able to get the arrest off Mark's record with community service activities."

"Very good. See, that's how accessing your network can help resolve problems."

"Yes, and I was thinking about how Mark and I might do the community service together. It would give us time together without feeling any pressure to talk."

"Great idea! That would allow your conversations to flow more naturally. Making more time together would help you bond better and improve communications. That's why time is listed as a resource also."

"That's always been a tough one for me. With me trying to stay ahead at work, my time at home and for other activities has always been limited."

"I think a lot of people don't realize the value of time. Relationships take time to develop, and most elements of life are best realized when shared with others."

"I am beginning to appreciate that."

"You know, community service would also fall into the category of body and mind," Randy stated.

"How do you mean?" Joe asked.

"You and Mark performing community service is a great way to use your body and mind to help others in a very positive way. Plus, it fosters good feelings that lead to positive mental and emotional health."

"I see your point. Some of the community service activities are physically active. Habitat for Humanity, for example, can involve a lot of physical labor. I know I often feel better about myself after I have been physically active, whether it's exercise or yard work."

"And when you feel better about yourself, you tend to have more energy to solve life's problems."

Randy added a little red wine to each of their glasses with a satisfied smile. Joe's face no longer appeared as heavy, and his eyes had a slight sparkle. Joe offered a smile in return and took a sip of wine, feeling a little less burdened. The waiter served both men their Caesar salads and offered fresh ground pepper. The salads looked amazing, and Joe was pretty hungry by now, but his thoughts were far from his appetite. Randy's words had struck a chord with him. Joe had begun to realize his life needed to change, and he was beginning to envision a path heading in the right direction.

"So, Randy, I understand networking, time, and body and mind as resources that help me overcome problems in my life," Joe said. "And I see how each one can help me be a better parent for Mark. Tell me what wisdom and talents mean on your list."

"You're a successful attorney, Joe, and you have experienced a lot in life," Randy said. "That automatically means you have wisdom and talents that you can use to help you."

"Funny, I don't feel very wise or talented at the moment. Everything seems to be going awry."

"Don't be silly. We all have our ups and downs. In fact, it's during life's struggles when we often gain the most wisdom and realize our greatest talents."

"That's probably true. I remember how grueling law school was, but my learning curve was incredibly steep during those years."

"Exactly. So what wisdom and talents do you have today that could help you be a better parent for Mark?"

"As far as talents, I am very organized and am a good writer. Mark does have college applications coming up, and I could help him tackle those."

"That's true. And it would again increase the time you spend together. What about pieces of wisdom?"

"Well, I've made my own share of mistakes in my life. I've gotten into trouble with my parents when I was in high school because I got drunk at a friend's house. I didn't get arrested, but the mistake was still the same."

"Then you two have something in common."

"I know Mark is a good kid, and he probably got drunk because he's dealing with a lot of things in his life. In the grand scheme of things, this will not be a big deal. Mark just needs to know we all make mistakes and that, no matter what, I will always love him."

"That's definitely a piece of wisdom you should share with him."

"And I can tell Mark how proud I am that he decided to walk home rather than get in the car with someone who was drunk."

"Exactly. Even in his drunken condition, he displayed good judgment. By showing him that he's not alone in making mistakes and sharing life's wisdom with him, you will open the door for better communication. That's how wisdom can be a resource and contribute to one's true wealth."

"It's funny, Randy, but I know I am probably gaining a lot of wisdom right now that will help me later in life. With you, the marriage counselor, and my family, I am gaining a new perspective on things important to me."

"You mean you're realizing what your priorities really are?"

"Yeah, I guess so. Knowing your priorities is wisdom in itself, and that can be a huge support when trying to figure out the best solution to a problem."

"Couldn't have said it better myself," Randy said, grinning. "For most of us to make significant changes in our lives, we must first experience intense pain. It's almost as if the pain acts as a sledgehammer to break our old destructive patterns so that we can move towards a healthier and happier future."

Randy and Joe took a few more bites of their salads in silence while soft jazz echoed throughout the restaurant. Joe hadn't noticed the music previously, but the serenity provided by the instrumental songs, along with the soft glow of the tableside lanterns, made him feel very relaxed and peaceful. The feeling had been a rarity over the past few months, and he relished it as he slowly ate his salad. It was too bad the feeling wouldn't last, but at least for the moment he felt content.

"We've talked about time, body and mind, wisdom, talents, and networking," Joe recapped. "We haven't talked about money as a resource for wealth. I would have thought that would have been the most important."

"You're not alone," Randy said. "Most people would agree with you."

"Especially with you being a financial advisor, I would have expected that to be the main element of true wealth."

"In reality, money is often just a supporting tool for the other resources we talked about. For example, money is needed to pay for an attorney to help Mark with his legal problems. Money will help pay the fees for college applications. But when we confront specific challenges, money is often more of a supporting resource rather than a primary one."

"Are you telling me that more money doesn't make me an overall wealthier person?" Joe asked.

"More money makes you financially wealthier, but depending on what you do to acquire the money and how you spend it, it may or may not make your true wealth rise. We all need money to meet our basic needs," Randy clarified. "But after a certain point, when our basic needs are met, money doesn't necessarily add much unless used to enhance other elements of our lives."

"Okay, I'm lost. You don't think that if I earn three hundred thousand dollars a year instead of two hundred thousand dollars a year, I wouldn't be happier and wealthier?"

"You might be or you might not be. It depends on what role money plays in your life."

"It seems pretty clear to me that the more money you have, the more secure you are and the more freedom you have."

"That might seem clear to you, but I don't see it that way. Let me ask you a question. If your premise is right, does that mean that every day the stock market goes south, you are automatically less secure and less free?"

"Well, yeah…kinda. I mean if I have a lower net worth one day than I had the day before, then my financial future is less secure and I am less free. I have to work more to regain the same level of security."

"So even though we know the market is constantly going up and down and that these fluctuations are temporary, you still believe you have more or less security with each change. Do you feel less secure when you eat a nice meal out at Mickey's? Essentially your net worth drops when you spend money, too."

"I understand your point, but to a degree money means greater security," Joe stated, refusing to relinquish his point.

"There's an element of truth there," Randy conceded, "but once we have enough money for shelter, clothing, food, transportation, and other relative comforts, having more money does not necessarily mean more security, freedom, happiness, or even wealth."

"Last year I dreamed about buying a Jaguar convertible. With an unknown financial future looming overhead, now I dream about a Prius. How is that wealthier and more secure?"

"Security and wealth don't just come from money, Joe. True wealth and security come from many other things as well. All the things we have talked about tonight go into true wealth and security. The more wisdom, networking relationships, time, physical and mental health, and talents we enjoy, the wealthier we are."

"And the more money a person has also contributes to wealth."

"It does, but by itself money falls short. Instead of thinking of money as a means to greater security, it's better to think of it as a tool…a resource."

"A tool? What do you mean?"

"If money is a tool, you can do one of five things with it. One of these five is semi-voluntary, and the other four voluntary."

"Okay, I'll bite. What is the semi-voluntary one?"

"Paying taxes is the semi-voluntary thing we can do with money."

"That I'll agree with…unfortunately. What are the four voluntary things?"

"Well," Randy said as he began ticking off his fingers one by one, "one, you can invest it to create a more powerful tool; two, you can spend it to create the life you desire; three, you can use it to enhance the lives of the people you love; and, four, you can use it to support the causes you care about."

"Hmm," Joe uttered, rubbing his chin.

"Can you think of anything else you can do with money?" Randy asked.

"Well, addicts use money to feed their addiction. When a coke addict buys cocaine, I don't think it fits into any of those categories."

"The addict defines a better life as getting that short-term high. His intent is to live a better life as he defines it."

"I guess that's true. So of the four voluntary things you can do with money, only one generates greater financial wealth."

"That's right, but all the voluntary uses of money have the potential to generate greater true wealth. The difference is in how you define wealth."

Joe lifted his glass of wine to allow the waiter to clear his salad plate from the table.

"Your steaks will be out momentarily," the waiter stated. "Did you enjoy your salads, gentlemen?"

"It was excellent," Randy replied.

"Yes, it was very good," Joe added.

Satisfied, the waiter turned and walked away as Randy freshened both of their wine glasses with the remainder of the bottle. Joe adjusted his position in the chair and looked around the room as if to examine the décor. Randy had certainly touched upon a sensitive subject, and Joe realized he placed too much importance on money as a means to security. Readjusting his view was proving more difficult than he anticipated.

"I guess I'm just having trouble seeing money as a tool rather than the actual goal," Joe admitted. "For me, money has always meant greater safety and greater opportunity. It's one of the reasons I have worked so hard most of my life."

"I understand," Randy said. "This is a big paradigm shift. Money is important in providing many things, including opportunities. But money isn't necessarily synonymous with wealth. I have clients who are extremely rich but are miserable. They might be financially wealthy but I don't think anyone would say they were truly wealthy."

"So money is simply a tool to gain the things that are most important in our lives."

"Although it seems contradictory, money can be both the most powerful and the least powerful of the six elements. Money is the most powerful because it's the easiest to convert into the other five, but it's also the least powerful because money by itself solves very few problems."

"I understand," Joe said thoughtfully.

"As long as we define money as security or freedom, we stay in a place of fear. Because we fear money may be lost, we limit our lives and our options, desperately trying to hold on to what we have. But if you can cultivate a sense of security based upon what's inside you—your skills and talents, your intelligence, your persistence, your resilience, support of family and friends, and maybe even your faith in

God—you will open yourself up to new possibilities. This is where true wealth begins."

"Thanks, Randy. This has been really eye-opening for me," Joe said, raising his glass as if to toast Randy.

"I'm really glad, Joe. Trust me, you're not alone. Misunderstanding the purpose of money in attaining true wealth is one of the most common barriers to using your wealth to build a more meaningful and satisfying life."

"Here are your steaks, gentlemen," the waiter boasted proudly as the aroma of grilled tenderloin overtook the small table.

"Now, that's worth the wait," Randy stated, inhaling the steak's aroma and reaching for his fork and knife. "Pardon me, Joe, if my attention is consumed for the next several minutes or so."

"Hey, no problem," Joe replied. "I think this steak might be the seventh element to true wealth. What do you think?"

"You might just be right," Randy said with a big grin.

SEPTEMBER:
LIFE IS DIFFICULT

"If we can find a way to hold and embrace our pain gently, recognizing that brokenness is simply part of the human condition—in a sense, nothing special—than we may begin to feel empathically connected to all other beings. This is the broken heart that makes us whole."

—Estelle Frankel, *Sacred Therapy*

By all accounts, summer was over. Fall semester had begun and college football was in full swing. Winter fashions were already appearing in storefront displays and, before long, Halloween merchandise would consume a large part of many stores. But despite these telltale signs, the weather refused to say goodbye to summer. As Joe locked his car and headed for the diner, he could already feel the thick, heavy blanket of Georgia humidity engulf him. After having spent the last two weeks wrestling with his new situation, the feeling gave him a strange comfort. He, too, was not ready for a new season.

The tiny red brick building that housed Melissa's Diner was sandwiched between two multi-story office buildings in the heart of downtown Atlanta. The small piece of real estate it occupied was worth far more than the building itself, but as a breakfast landmark, it was priceless. The diner had long been known as the place for breakfast, and Joe was pleased when Randy suggested they meet here instead of their usual spot. Their French toast, seasoned with a perfect blend of cinnamon and powdered sugar, was one of Joe's weaknesses.

As Joe walked through the single glass door to the diner, he spotted Randy seated by himself with his eyes glued to his laptop. He seemed hard at work, punching the keyboard two fingers at a time with sleeves rolled up to his elbows. With his coffee mug nearly empty, it was evident Randy had been sitting there for a little while.

"Hard at work, I see," Joe said as he sat down across from his friend.

"Mornin', Joe," Randy replied, adding a couple of final taps to the computer before folding it shut. "I've got a deadline this morning and was wrapping up some details."

"If you need a little more time, I have a *Wall Street Journal* I could read," Joe offered.

"No, I'm fine. Thanks, though."

"So, how was your trip to Spain?"

"Absolutely perfect. Laura, the kids, and I spent two weeks there, and the weather was great. We spent a week in Barcelona then split the rest of the time among Madrid, Seville, and Toledo."

"That sounds wonderful. What did you like the most?"

"It might sound strange, but my favorite part of the trip was when we all played gin rummy each evening. The simplicity of just enjoying each other's company was really special. It was nice having the time to be together away from life's usual responsibilities."

"That doesn't sound odd to me at all. In fact, it sounds really nice." Joe looked wistful.

"How have you been since Mickey's? Any life-changing events?"

"Let's refill your cup of coffee before we get into that."

"Uh-oh. That sounds ominous."

Joe didn't reply but his face didn't refute Randy's observation. Raising his hand slightly, Joe was able to get the waitress' attention, and she headed toward their table, grabbing a pot of coffee on her way.

"Would you like some coffee?" the waitress asked Joe as she refilled Randy's cup.

"Yes, please," Joe replied.

"Are you gentlemen having breakfast as well?"

"Yes, we are," Joe stated. "Randy, do you know what you're having?"

"French toast for me," Randy replied. "I'm going with a sure thing."

"Me, too," Joe added.

"All right, two orders of French toast. Any bacon or sausage with that?" the waitress asked.

"Not for me," Randy replied.

"No, I'm good, too," Joe said. "Thanks."

The waitress collected both menus as Randy and Joe added cream to their coffees. Randy felt a little insensitive mentioning how he had enjoyed the family time on vacation considering what Joe had been going through lately. He hadn't intended to hurt Joe's feelings, but the thoughtful look on Joe's face suggested he had. After a minute's silence, Randy spoke.

"Okay, Joe," Randy said. "What's been going on with you?"

"It's been interesting since the last time we talked," Joe started. "I've been pretty busy at the firm doing a lot of work for Wind Technologies while trying to keep up with the demands of my other clients. I have been thinking a lot about balancing my time better, but that's easier said than done."

"Change takes time. Remember, changes occur incrementally. Baby steps."

"Well, despite trying to make sure I am spending enough time at home with Mark, on a few occasions I have still had to work into the night."

"Any complaints from Mark?"

"No, but then again he's a senior now. Not too many seniors complain their dad's not around to hang out with."

"That's true."

"Still, I know the more time I'm around, the more likely he'll open up to me. Anyway, one night last week I had to meet an out-of-town client at Julie's Grill for a working dinner."

"Nice place. I love their food."

"Yeah, me, too. So I met my client at the restaurant at seven and we began to discuss his business and some legal issues he's concerned about. Everything was going smoothly, but then, all of a sudden, I got one of the biggest shocks of my life."

"What? Did you get a call about Mark?"

"No. As I was in mid-sentence, out of the corner of my eye, I see Fran walk into Julie's with another guy."

"With a date?" Randy asked incredulously. "Did you know him?"

"No, I'd never seen him before in my life. They walked in on the other side of the restaurant, and he pulled out her chair for her as they sat down. She looked happier than I remember seeing her in a long time."

"Oh, boy…that had to be a hard pill to swallow."

"That's an understatement. The shock must have shown on my face, too, because my client asked if something was wrong."

"What did you say?"

"I told him the truth because I didn't think I could hide it. Plus, we've known each other a pretty long time. I excused myself to the restroom, where I splashed some cold water on my face and tried to regroup."

"Did it work?"

"It helped, but I still felt incredibly off-balance. All the confidence had been sucked out of me. My head was swimming and my hands were physically shaking as I walked back to the table."

"Did Fran see you?"

"Not for a while. She was too engrossed in conversation, or so it seemed."

"That doesn't sound like Fran."

"I know. She is usually the observant one. That made me feel even worse."

"How did the rest of the meal go?"

"Somehow I managed to get through my client meeting on task. Inside, I felt pretty surreal. Words were coming out of my mouth that made sense, but my head was a long way from our conversation. All I could think about was how bizarre everything was. Here was my wife of more than two decades sitting a few feet away from me with another man."

"Wow. That's a really strange situation to be in."

"You know, Randy, Fran was looking at this guy the way she used to look at me. It really stung to see it. I thought if I ever saw her with someone, I would get angry, but the truth is I was more hurt and humbled than anything."

Joe choked a little on his words and quickly took a sip of coffee to disguise any evidence of being upset. The sip was not quite as refreshing as the first few, but it served its purpose.

"That's really tough. I can imagine the strangeness of the whole scene, but it sounds like you handled it pretty well. At least you didn't make a big scene."

"Not at Julie's anyway."

"What do you mean?"

"I got home around nine-thirty, and Mark had left me a note telling me he was at his friend's house studying for a physics exam. I checked on him to see what time he was coming home, and then turned on the TV to distract my thoughts. Unfortunately, that didn't work. I began to feel resentful about everything. Fran was living in our house and going out on dates while I was stuck all alone in a crappy apartment."

"Did you call her again?"

"Worse. I got in my car and drove over to the house. The more I thought about how hard I was working to save our marriage, the angrier I got. Going to marriage counseling, refocusing my priorities, trying to understand what went wrong...I was trying, but I didn't see her making any effort at all. Fran had already made up her mind that our marriage was done."

"So what did you do?"

"I pulled up to the house and banged on the door."

"I'm hoping her date wasn't there."

"No, thank God. Fran answered the door, and I just stood there. I was almost too angry to speak. Finally, she asked me what I wanted, and that opened up the flood gates. I told her I wanted my life back, my house back, and my family back. And I told her she had a lot of nerve seeing somebody else when we were still going to counseling."

"Knowing Fran, I'm sure she didn't just take it. How did she react?"

"She told me I should have thought about what I wanted a long time ago. She said the man was a friend who she had met in art class, and, unlike me, he listened to what she had to say and paid attention to her."

"That had to hurt."

"It did. But instead of showing how hurt I was I began yelling. I don't know…something just snapped. I called her ungrateful and spoiled rotten. I told her that not only was she running around town with other men, but she continued to live a life of luxury that I provided for her. While I was out working like a dog, she was prancing around town with any man she could find."

"Joe, that's pretty rough. That doesn't even sound like something you would say."

"I know. Fran's eyes began to well with tears. I knew as soon as I said it, it was a huge mistake. I felt like a real heel. She told me I needed to leave and that as far as she was concerned, the marriage was over."

"Did you leave?"

"I didn't have a lot of choice. She slammed the door in my face. Even though I knocked for several minutes, she wouldn't answer the door again. I finally got in my car and went back to my apartment, feeling even worse than I did before."

"I am so sorry, Joe."

The smell of cinnamon and sugar interrupted their conversation as the waitress arrived with two warm plates of French toast. Both of them paused long enough to place their napkins in their laps and pour maple syrup onto their toast, but Randy had lost a bit of his excitement about breakfast having heard Joe's story. Joe unenthusiastically took a bite and ate methodically, barely noticing the richness of the flavor. Compared to the dinner he and Randy had had last month, this meal seemed very bland. In fact, nothing seemed very appealing to Joe in the last week.

"Have you talked to Fran since then?" Randy asked in between bites.

"As luck would have it, we had our next marriage counseling session two days later," Joe replied. "I wasn't sure if Fran would show up, but she did."

"How did it go?"

"Neither one of us spoke at first. Helen, our counselor, asked some questions that opened things up a bit. But when I tried to talk about what had happened at the restaurant, Fran interrupted me and said she had something to say."

"I think I know where this is going."

"Fran said she had made up her mind that she no longer wanted to be married to me and that she wanted a divorce."

"Were you surprised?"

"Not really, after the other night. The way she looked at the guy told me a lot. But that didn't stop me from trying one last time to save our marriage."

"What did you do?"

"I told Fran how sorry I was about the things I had said and that I had something to show her. I pulled out my list of priorities and explained that what mattered most to me was my relationship with her, being a good dad for the kids, being healthy, and having close friendships. I told her I was committed to making a change with these in mind."

"That's really great, Joe. How did Fran react?"

"She smiled at me for the first time in a while, like a mother would if she were proud of her son. But she said it was too late for us. She admitted that she developed feelings for Ron, the guy on the date with her. She said she had made her decision."

"I'm still glad you shared your list of priorities with her. Even though it didn't seem to make a big difference in healing your marriage, it may help a lot down the road."

"I can't see down the road, Randy. All I can see is what's happening right now. I tried one more time to talk her out of her decision. I suggested her attraction to Ron might just be an attraction to a life free of the stress and pain we'd been experiencing lately. I reminded her we once shared a connection and that we could reestablish that connection again. I begged her to give it another try."

"And?"

"She began to cry, but she still said no. I'm sure it was a tough moment for her, but I definitely know it was tough for me."

"How did the session end?"

"At that point, Helen said what we already knew. She told us further sessions weren't needed, but she offered to help us in telling Marcia and Mark about the decision to divorce. Then she told us that we should both get a divorce attorney and try to work things out between us without going to court, if possible."

"Sounds like good advice."

"Yeah, it was. It surprised me, though, that Fran said she already had an attorney."

"I guess Fran's mind was definitely made up."

"I'd say. Helen told me I should get an attorney as well and that I should also consider seeing a therapist."

"That's not a bad idea either. I remember when I went through my divorce, my therapist really helped me. She made me realize things I never would have realized alone. These are the types of resources of support that you can use to help with life's problems. All too often, people wait too late to take advantage of professionals."

"I don't know. I asked Helen if she would be able to provide individual counseling, but she felt like she would be a better resource for both of us together should we need to return as a couple or as parents. I don't really want to tell my story all over again to someone new...plus I have you."

"Whoa," Randy said, raising his hands. "I am happy to share some wisdom and experiences with you, Joe, but I am a far cry from a therapist. You need someone who can professionally understand the emotional roller coaster you're on and all the stresses that go with it."

"Yeah, I'm sure you're right, but you've helped me a great deal."

"I am happy to be your friend and your financial advisor, but when it comes to things like this, I think professional therapy is the way to go. What we talk about doesn't replace that."

"Yeah, you're right. I guess I am just a little exhausted and seeing another therapist feels a little overwhelming."

The morning rush was now in full swing, and several people were now waiting for seats at the front of the diner. The young waitress had waited to collect their plates, noticing that Joe's plate was still nearly full, but the crowd pushed her to reconsider.

"Would either of you care for more coffee or should I just bring your check?" the waitress asked as she collected Randy's plate.

"A little more coffee, please," Randy replied.

"Are you still working on your French toast?" she asked, turning to Joe.

"I think I'm done," Joe said. "Just not too hungry today."

Randy looked over at Joe and noticed the heavy bags under his eyes. Joe sat somewhat slumped over in his chair, taking a sip of his coffee and looking out the adjacent window. From what Randy could tell, Joe didn't appear to be looking at anything in particular, and his flat expression made him look ghostly.

"How are you doing, Joe?" Randy asked in an empathetic tone.

"I've been better," Joe replied without breaking his stare outside. "I left Helen's office and remember noticing that the sun was still shining and people were still going about their regular business. Nothing seemed to have changed on the outside. But my world had changed forever…it was a strange feeling."

"You've been through a lot this month, not to mention everything you've already dealt with since May. Any change in life can be tough, but the types of changes you are going through are some of the toughest."

"I just don't feel very confident about anything anymore. I used to feel like I had it all together, but now I'm not even sure I can balance a checkbook. It just seems like everything collapsed so quickly."

"Confidence doesn't come from things that happen on the outside. Confidence comes from within. Do you remember talking about faith and gratitude?"

"Yes. Are you saying I should be thankful for my divorce?"

"No, I'm not, but rarely is anything in life all bad or all good. Your separation from Fran has been painful, but at the same time it has made you realize some things."

"Such as?"

"Such as your real priorities in life. You have a clearer idea of what is most important to you. Do you think we would have been talking about your priorities if you and Fran weren't having problems?"

"Probably not."

"You don't have to be grateful for your divorce, but you can have faith that some positive things will come of it. When you have faith and find things to be thankful for, you automatically feel more confident. And when you feel more confident, you make better decisions."

"That's a tough one. I am having a hard time seeing anything I should be thankful for at the moment."

"That's okay. You don't have to see anything right now. Just be open to the idea that some positive things will come out of this. Are you and Mark closer than you were a few months ago?"

"We are. He's been sharing things with me about school and about his interests lately. He never did that before."

"So that's a positive, right? That's something to be thankful for. Why do you think that happened?"

"For one, I am spending more time with Mark."

"How is Mark doing, by the way?"

"His court date is set for October, but my friend Perry is pretty confident he can get the arrest off his record with some community service."

"So you've reached out to your network of friends to help Mark with his problems."

"I have."

"And you're also closer to your brother and sister, right?"

"That's true. They've been really supportive over the last few months. I'm beginning to see your point."

"All I am saying is that even the bad stuff in life can have some positives. If you have faith and gratitude, focus on your most important priorities, and use your resources along the way, you can make it through life's challenges. These are the things that give you confidence, which, in turn, helps you make wise decisions each step of the way."

Randy swallowed the last sip of coffee and waved to the waitress to come over with the check. Joe finished his coffee as well and neatly folded his napkin onto the table.

"Here's your check, gentlemen. Hopefully you'll bring your appetite next time," the waitress said teasingly, turning mid-sentence towards Joe.

"That's usually not a problem," Joe replied, patting his belly.

"This should cover the check," Randy said, handing the waitress some money.

"I'll be right back with your change," she replied.

"That's all right. We're all set," Randy said with a pleasant smile.

"Thank you very much. You both have a great day."

"Randy, you didn't have to get breakfast. Thanks for doing that," Joe said.

"Don't sweat it. After the week you've had, you certainly deserve a free breakfast," Randy replied.

"I hardly even asked about you. What's going on in your life?"

"Well, the vacation was great, but I've had some struggles lately, too. Mine haven't been nearly as overwhelming as yours, but my dad was diagnosed with early prostate cancer since we last talked."

"Really? I'm sorry to hear that."

"Yeah. The doctor said it was detected early, and because it's slow-growing, it isn't likely to be anything serious at my father's age."

"How old is your dad?"

"He's eighty. The doctor said he would likely die of something else before the cancer caused any problems. I must say my dad didn't find that too comforting."

"Not the best bedside manner, huh? I'm sorry to hear that. How's your mom taking the news?"

"She's a pretty nervous person anyway, so she's always thinking the worst. I think she fears that my dad will die first, leaving her all alone."

"I understand what you're going through. I lost my dad a few years ago."

"It's just part of life. As we get older, so do our parents, and there comes a time for us to help take care of them. I've been very lucky. Not only have they been wonderful parents, but they've always enjoyed excellent health. I am thankful for the opportunity to help them for a change."

"I understand completely."

"Have you read *The Road Less Traveled* by Scott Peck? It is one of my favorite books. The first three words of the book are 'Life is difficult.' Peck says the more we realize that life is difficult, the easier life will be for us. Joe, we both have our own challenges, but we'll get through them, and we'll be stronger and wiser from the experience."

"As always, thanks for your friendship, Randy."

"My pleasure, Joe. We're on for next month as usual?"

"I wouldn't miss it. Have a good week and good luck with your parents."

"Have a good week yourself. Remember…look for the positives."

Randy and Joe shook hands, and Joe made his way to the door while Randy packed up his laptop. He squeezed past the patrons at the front patiently waiting for a table, and walked out into the warm morning sun. For a moment he paused and looked up and down the block. The sun was still shining, and people were still going about their regular routines. That hadn't changed. But Joe knew his life had, and it was up to him to find his way through the struggles that lay ahead. Life was indeed difficult, but he knew he had many things for which to be thankful.

OCTOBER: THE COMFORTS OF HAPPINESS

Don't confuse pleasure with happiness, and never exchange happiness for pleasure.

—David Geller

Crack! The sound of the wooden bat striking the ball immediately grabbed the attention of thousands of fans just in time to see it launch toward right center field. The midday sun obscured the ball's visibility momentarily, but there was little doubt it had cleared the fence as Braves' stadium erupted in applause and cheers. Having just taken their seats behind home plate, Randy and Joe couldn't have timed it any better. They had arrived just in time to see the Braves score their first run of the day.

"Great seats," Randy said, examining their panoramic view of the field.

"I know," Joe replied. "The firm usually gives these tickets out to clients, but considering the Braves might be in the playoffs, I put dibs on some end-of-season tickets."

"I'm glad you did. It's a great day for a baseball game."

"I'm glad you approve. I always said it's important to keep your financial advisor happy," Joe said with a grin.

Joe and Randy both settled into their seats, trying to balance the classic baseball meal in their hands: a hotdog, peanuts, and an ice-cold beer. A soft breeze blew across the field, complementing the warm sunshine of the autumn day. Despite it being nearly the last game of the regular season, very few seats were vacant. Postseason excitement was already in the air.

"So what's up?" Joe asked in between bites of his hot dog. "You're almost never late."

"I know," Randy replied. "Sorry about that. I was on the phone with one of my long-term clients, and I just couldn't break away."

"Anything serious?"

"Not in reality. But if you asked him, he would say the world is coming to an end."

"What do you mean?"

"Well, he and his wife have been clients of mine for a long time, and honestly he's built a nice portfolio that's well invested. Even though he's in great shape, he freaks out every time the market drops."

"So you had to talk him down from his anxiety?"

"Yeah, which wouldn't be so bad if it occurred occasionally. But lately it's been happening more often."

"Why do you think that is?"

"My gut feeling is he's thinking about retirement as he approaches sixty-five, and he's panicking about what to do next. When he worries about the market and his money, he distracts himself from his real concerns and rationalizes why he has to keep working."

"I see. So you think he's really worried about how to fill his time when he retires."

"Maybe. He has always been a workaholic, and perhaps he just doesn't know what he'll do with his time. He's always talked about it and seemed to be looking forward to it, but now that the day of retirement approaches, he might be unsure."

"Strike three; you're out!" screamed the home-plate umpire, who was well within hearing distance.

Both Joe and Randy took a sip of their beers as the Reds swapped their positions on the field with the Braves. The cool beer was quite refreshing and perfect for a Saturday afternoon.

Joe identified each of the familiar faces of the Braves as they walked onto the field. A new face was on third base that Joe didn't recognize. He knew the regular third baseman, Chipper Jones, had been on the injured list, however. He wondered what the young kid now playing third base thought about being in the Big Show.

"A wise man once told me change is difficult," Joe commented. "I'm nowhere close to retirement, but I can appreciate feeling a bit unsettled about not working."

"Change is hard, and you've had your fair share," Randy added. "How are things with you?"

"As you might expect, lots has happened in the last month. Fran and I haven't talked much at all, and we both have settled into a temporary routine. It still feels very surreal."

"Did you tell the kids about the divorce?"

"Actually, no. Fran and I decided not to tell them until Marcia comes home for winter break. We just didn't want to upset her in the middle of the semester. I still have Mark every other week, and I'm not sure what he thinks about everything. He certainly knows Fran and I aren't communicating very well."

"Don't you and Mark talk?"

"We talk about a lot of things, but I avoid talking about my issues with Fran. I don't want to put him in the middle."

"What about Marcia? Have you talked to her?"

"Definitely. She calls me or I call her at least once a week. She wants to know how marriage counseling is going and is always asking how I am doing in the apartment. I avoid the details about counseling, but I'm pretty open with her about the rest of my life."

"And she's handling all of this pretty well?"

"After her initial blow-up, she seems to be handling it okay. Don't get me wrong. She definitely wants her parents back together, and I suspect she still blames me for working too much. But she's a realist, too, and she has a big heart."

"That's good to hear. Maybe she'll handle the news of the divorce well, too. If she's a realist, she probably suspects it's coming anyway."

"Yeah, maybe. I know she'll be fine. I just hate disappointing her."

Joe polished off the last bite of his hot dog and opened a bag of roasted peanuts. The familiar tastes of the ballpark and the game's pleasant pace made him feel relaxed. The atmosphere was quite different from the hustle and bustle of the work week. It also provided a haven away from his apartment, where he was too frequently reminded of all the problems in his life. Even if the game only lasted a few hours, the escape was much appreciated.

"Did you think about seeing a therapist?" Randy asked.

"As a matter of fact, I did," Joe replied. "I must confess the way I got there wasn't necessarily purposeful, but I got there all the same."

"What do you mean?"

"Well, I haven't been sleeping that great, so I went to my regular doctor for some sleeping medicine. When he gave me the prescription, he insisted I see a psychologist because he thought my insomnia was related to stress."

"Can't argue that one."

"I know. So I saw a psychologist named Josh Smith. When I first went into his office, I almost turned around and left. I honestly didn't think I needed any therapy. I'm not happy about all the stuff going on in my life, but I'm handling it okay. The whole thing just seemed like a waste of time."

"So what happened?"

"I stayed, and I must say I'm glad I did. Josh asked me some basic questions to get the conversation rolling, and, before I knew it, I was telling him my frustrations, disappointments, and worries. I think out of the entire hour, I talked all but five minutes."

"That's great. It's amazing how much you can open up with a good therapist. It sounds like that's what you needed."

"I guess so. Anyway, I saw him again the next week, too. I think the more I see him, the better it will be. He's still just getting to know me right now."

"It does take some time to see the benefits but, as unmanly as it sounds, just expressing your feelings can be a tremendous help."

"That's what I'm realizing. It's also good to know that I'm not the first guy to experience all the pains and emotions I'm feeling."

"Absolutely."

The crowd around Joe and Randy suddenly stood as a foul ball had managed to sneak behind the home plate netting and strike a few seats away from them. A teenage boy snagged the errant ball with his glove in the midst of several would-be souvenir collectors. The boy smiled ear to ear, proud of his accomplishment and prize, and then enjoyed the replay of his catch on the Jumbotron.

"Nice catch," Joe commented. "I bet Mark could have made that catch, too."

"What's going on with Mark and his court date?"

"Lots, actually. I think I mentioned that my friend Perry Stevens is Mark's attorney. Among other things, Perry suggested Mark and I attend an Alcoholic Anonymous meeting together."

"Really? Is Mark having problems with alcohol I don't know about?"

"No, but Perry and I talked about Mark's behavior that night and how it might relate to school stress and our marriage troubles. He thought it might be good for Mark to see the negative effects of alcohol. At the same time, he thought it might not hurt his case with the D.A."

"So did you two go to a meeting?"

"We did. I'll tell you, Randy...it was pretty powerful. Mark and I went to one for teens and young adults, and the stories were amazing. The battles these kids have had with alcohol and their fight to take back control of their lives made a huge impression on Mark and me."

"That's a great experience for Mark. And it's great you guys went together."

"It really was. If nothing else, Mark was able to see how using alcohol to escape life's pressures can really cause bigger problems. It helped me understand what can happen to kids during stressful times if they don't get the support they need from their family."

"Maybe that will help his court case as well."

"Perry also suggested that Mark complete forty hours of community service prior to his court date, which has now been moved to January. If he does, the D.A. has agreed to drop the charges against him."

"That's a huge blessing."

"Definitely. But what's even more of a blessing is the community service itself."

"What do you mean?"

"Mark and I talked about what kind of community service he would like to do, and I told him I would do it with him. So he thought helping out at a homeless shelter would be an experience he would like."

"Mark's a special kid."

"I think so. Anyway, we decided to volunteer at Helping Hands, which is a homeless shelter for mothers and children. This past Saturday was our first time. Have you ever worked at a shelter?"

"My temple volunteers at a shelter every winter," Randy said. "And Debbie, my ex-wife, and I made lasagnas and served them at a shelter about five years ago. It was really a rewarding experience. I'm not sure why I never did it again."

"You got busy like the rest of us. Anyway, the whole day was a real eye-opener for me," Joe continued. "I've always realized how fortunate I am to have the lifestyle I do, but seeing the mothers and children in the shelter really opened my eyes."

"I'm sure you gained a new perspective on things."

"I really did. After we served dinner and cleaned up, Mark and I sat and talked with a young woman named Christy. I'd guess she's in her mid-twenties, and she has a four-year-old and a six-month-old."

"That's tough. She lives at the shelter?'

"Yeah, with both children. She told us stories about when she was homeless. Some of them were hard to hear, but some were actually amusing. Despite her hardships and lack of money, Christy is determined to clean up her act and take care of her kids. I was really moved, and I could see that Mark was also."

"How so?"

"I see myself worrying about money all the time and complaining about my problems, but compared to Christy, I've got it made."

"You know, I have a client from India who lives in Atlanta now. He always says he wakes up and realizes he's better off than ninety-five percent of the rest of the world. He is so right, yet it's easy to lose perspective about how good we have it."

"You're right. I asked Bruce Shaw, the director of Helping Hands, about Christy, and he said she'd been battling addiction to drugs since she was thirteen years old. She's been clean now for three months and just got a job at Target with the shelter's help. Christy's goal is to save enough for her own apartment, but it's not easy with a terrible credit score and a minimum-wage job."

"Especially with two kids."

"I know. If that doesn't make you feel thankful for what you have, I'm not sure what will."

Again, the crowd jumped to its feet as two Braves base runners sped around the bases. A line drive up the middle had provided Atlanta with an opportunity to take the lead, and everyone cheered as the second runner streaked across home plate a split second before the ball arrived in the catcher's mitt. Applause erupted, and Joe and Randy stood and cheered as well. Then, slowly, everyone sat back in their seats, satisfied with the current state of affairs. Joe smiled thinking how such little things as a baseball game could make so many people temporarily happy.

"You know, Randy," Joe said thoughtfully, "the one person who most intrigued me was Bruce Shaw, the director."

"Why is that?"

"The entire day Mark and I were at the shelter, Bruce was always upbeat and positive regardless of the situation. He seemed genuinely happy."

"Why is that so intriguing?"

"I don't know. I know Bruce couldn't possibly make a lot of money, and he's constantly dealing with people who are struggling to get by. He seems to give so much of himself and get so little in return."

"So, why do you think Bruce is so happy? And why do you think he is getting so little in return for his efforts?"

"I'm not sure. I certainly felt very good after working at the shelter all day, but Bruce is there all the time. He doesn't have another job that pays him a big salary. He probably just earns enough to cover his bills, yet he seems happier than most of my partners at the firm. With our spacious homes, expensive cars, and luxury vacations, you'd expect us to be happier than Bruce."

"Let me ask you a question, Joe. Do you think more money means more happiness?"

"I know the old adage 'money doesn't buy happiness,' and I suppose I agree with it. However, money does make your life easier and gives you an opportunity to enjoy yourself."

"So, why is Bruce happier than your partners?"

"That's what I can't understand."

"Have we talked about the difference between happiness and pleasure?"

"No, but I am sure you are about to tell me," Joe said with a slight grin.

"Only if you want to hear it," Randy replied.

"I'm just kidding. I'm definitely interested."

"Pleasure is all about our senses. It is watching a beautiful sunset or having a wonderful meal at a great restaurant."

"Okay, I'll buy that."

"If we have the money, it is easy to use our money to increase our pleasure. You and your partners do that all the time."

"Okay, I'm still with you."

"Pleasure, however, is not happiness. Happiness is not only about having a comfortable lifestyle along with some fun, but it is also about the quality of our relationships, our ability to be fully engaged in life, and the chance to make a positive difference in the lives of others."

"All of those things sound great, but money still matters. I know for a fact that Christy would welcome more money so she could get an apartment and put food on the table. Are you telling me more money wouldn't make her happier?"

"No, I feel pretty confident more money would make Christy happier because it would meet her basic needs. In Christy's case, more money would allow her to have her own apartment, feed her family, provide her children basic health care, and so on. Depending on how much money she had, she might even have a little left over for some fun."

"So money does buy happiness."

"Only to a point. It's hard to be happy if you're worried about your basic needs. In Christy's case, more money allows her to meet those basic needs. Once those needs are met, increases in income generally don't provide a big increase in happiness."

"But wouldn't Christy be even happier if she lived in a mansion in a nice neighborhood?"

"She might or might not. If she lived in a mansion but felt isolated from her family, she would likely feel lonely and less happy."

"So you're saying even though my partners earn more money than Bruce, they're not happier than Bruce because Bruce has enough money for a comfortable lifestyle?"

"Exactly, and my hunch is Bruce is happier than your partners for reasons other than income. He likely receives greater happiness from his relationships and his level of engagement in life."

"But, Randy, if I earn more money and I'm able to travel or buy a new car, these things do make me happier."

"I'd say they give you pleasure. Don't get me wrong; pleasure is a good thing. But your partners get into trouble when they exchange happiness for pleasure, which is always a bad deal."

"What do you mean?"

"Pleasure is good. It's nice to eat at a great restaurant, live in a big home, or take a European cruise. But if you work sixty hours a week in a job you don't like for such things, you might not be happy. Pleasure is good, but happiness is great. Never exchange pleasure for happiness."

"Okay, I get your point."

"Research has found that up to the first one hundred thousand a year that people earn, the effects from this in providing a better lifestyle has significant effects on happiness. But whatever money we make in excess of this amount doesn't have much of an effect unless it's used to pursue the three key elements of happiness."

"And what were they again?"

"Having better relationships, being engaged, and making a difference in the lives of others."

Joe snapped a couple of peanuts in two and added to the pile of empty shells beneath his seat. He could see across the stadium that the crowd had begun to do "the wave," and he prepared to participate as it headed his way. Maybe Randy was right. Bruce did appear to be pretty happy. Despite all the human suffering he experienced on a daily basis, Bruce managed to smile, joke, and stay positive. Joe stood and raised his arms in the air along with Randy, who enthusiastically joined in. The wave was such a silly thing, but everyone smiled as they stood up and sat back down. Clearly, money wasn't everything.

"Wasn't there another part of the first element of happiness you mentioned?" Joe asked as he returned to his seat and his peanuts.

"Lifestyle and fun...that's the first element," Randy replied.

"I always thought fun and happiness were the same thing. But I guess they're not exactly the same."

"Fun is great, but fun and happiness are not the same thing. Fun is often related to pleasure. When's the last time you had fun?"

"I'm having fun right now," Joe replied.

"Me, too. Have you been having more fun in your life lately?"

"It's odd, but I'd have to say yes. I'm actually having more fun now than I did when I was at home with Fran. I'm definitely having fun spending more time with Mark, and working fewer hours has allowed me to do some things I really like."

"Such as?"

"I've been reading more lately. I forgot how much I enjoy reading about faraway places and travel. And since I started working less at night, I've found work more enjoyable, too."

"Having fun at your job is one of the greatest things in the world. And when we balance our time better between work and leisure, we have more energy and creative abilities in other areas of our lives."

"Maybe Bruce is just having more fun at Helping Hands than other people do in their jobs. He was playing Frisbee with a bunch of kids when Mark and I were there. He just looked like he was having a ball."

"Did Mark join in?"

"He did. I could tell Mark was having a good time all day. One of the kids was having some trouble in math at school, so Mark sat down with him and helped him for about an hour. Mark likes math and really enjoys teaching."

"That's great, Joe."

"Yeah. Mark told me on the way home it was his favorite part of the day."

"I know it sounds strange, but Mark's drinking incident may be a really good thing for both of you."

"I know. We had a really good day last weekend at Helping Hands, and I think we're both looking forward to going again."

"That's great. Sounds like you're making some good choices."

"Well, I have to be honest. I'm still nervous about finances and the divorce, Randy. I've worked hard to have the things I have, and I would like to retire and travel at a reasonable age."

"I understand, Joe. I just want you to remember that you're in great financial shape. Our financial models account for inflation, taxes, a wide range of economic and market scenarios, and assume you live to be one hundred years of age. Your portfolio has a nice mixture of cash, stocks, and bonds and is designed to give you the income you need while protecting you against inflation. I see no reason you won't be able to travel and retire at a reasonable age."

"I know what you're saying is right, but I guess I'm still nervous."

"Have you gotten an attorney yet?"

"I have. As you know, I had to put together financials for Fran's attorney last week. We're trying to work out the details collaboratively with Fran's attorney, but we'll see. I'm afraid of what might happen if things go south."

"Don't get ahead of yourself. It's in everyone's best interest to work this out collaboratively, and nothing you've said tells me Fran wants to take you to the cleaners. Just take things one day at a time. You're going to be okay."

"I hope so."

"It isn't a matter of hope. When you get nervous, I want you to think about Bruce Shaw."

"Why Bruce?"

"You just said Bruce was happier than most of your partners even though he has a lot less money. You have a lot more money than Bruce, and if he can be happy, so can you."

Suddenly, the familiar sound of the organ started playing the opening notes to "Take Me out to the Ball Game." Randy and Joe looked at each other, realizing they had been so immersed in their conversation they had nearly missed the entire game. But neither one really cared. Joe was simply having a fun time catching up with his friend and enjoying the peacefulness of a Saturday afternoon at a baseball game. It had been a great day.

"Hey, why don't we at least pay attention to the last couple of innings?" Joe suggested.

"Sounds like the right thing to do," Randy replied. "And maybe get another cold one."

"Excellent idea…my treat."

NOVEMBER: BECOMING ENGAGED IN LIFE

A great job reflects your life priorities, allows you to use your Signature Talents™, and has a culture that fits your work values.

The sun glimmered through the north Georgia pines onto the weathered dirt path now covered with leaves. The array of colors combined with the morning light created a vibrant atmosphere, and the crisp air heightened the senses. With backpacks in place, Joe led Randy along a narrow corridor of the woods, slowly making an ascent. The crunch of branches and leaves under their soles softly disrupted the silence of their surroundings, and the melodic rhythm created by their steady strides was a comfort to the soul.

"It's really peaceful here," Randy said, interrupting several minutes of silence. "You couldn't have picked a better morning to go hiking."

"Isn't that the truth?" Joe replied without slowing his pace. "I've wanted to get outdoors a bit more, and I haven't been to north Georgia in a while. Autumn is my favorite time of year."

"This is a nice change from the office. Just being here kind of recharges your batteries."

"I know what you mean. Years ago I would come here every couple of months just to relax, but with kids and all, life got busy. It seemed like I never had the time."

"Well, you made time today, and I'm glad you did," Randy said.

"Me, too."

The two continued to hike up the small mountain. The various trails had been marked with different spray-painted colors on the trees, and Joe was following the blue hash marks. Given the troubles in his life over the last several months, he thought the blue trail was most appropriate.

"So how are things going, Joe?" Randy asked as they both proceeded along the trail.

"I don't know," Joe replied in a somewhat melancholy voice. "I know things are better than they have been, but I just wish they would speed up a bit."

"What do you mean?"

"Remember that life priorities exercise we did a few months ago?"

"Of course."

"Well, only a few of them had to do with work. Most of them had to do with building relationships and creating more time for myself. I've made some positive changes in that direction, but not as much as I would like."

"What's keeping you from making a bigger change?"

"My financial situation, of course," Joe replied as he stopped hiking and turned his head around to look at Randy face to face. "Don't you remember telling me if I divorced I would be making some lifestyle adjustments?"

"I remember saying you might need to make some adjustments, but how is that keeping you from building better relationships and creating more time for yourself?" Randy replied somewhat defensively.

"If I lose my shirt in this divorce, I've got to work more to keep my financial footing. I can't afford to back off of work. In fact, I should be working harder," Joe said as he resumed hiking.

"That's where we don't see eye to eye."

"How can you not see that, Randy?"

"Your anxiety is getting the better of you. You're fearful because you imagine the worst possible outcome in the divorce. The fear then makes you feel restricted, burdened, and overwhelmed. I really urge you to think about the good things going on in your life, like the time you're spending with Mark. Focus on what you have faith in, or rely on, as you face an uncertain future."

"Okay, I understand. I do fear the worst. I just envision myself either having to work harder or going broke."

"I see a lot more options for you than those two."

"Like what?"

"You have lots of choices. For example, one option might include working less and working longer."

"I don't want to work forever."

"Who said anything about working forever? If memory serves me right, we assumed in your projections you would retire at the age of sixty. You always told me you wanted to retire and be able to live a life of leisure."

"That hasn't changed. I have worked incredibly hard for a really long time."

"I know you have, but have you considered what benefits work provides you beyond income?"

"Beyond income? Like what?"

"You enjoy being around other people. You enjoy learning and experiencing new things. Think about how you felt the other week when you helped that client sell their company. You probably feel a genuine sense of satisfaction in helping a client, right?"

"I do."

"My hunch is after a year or two of retirement, you'll be bored and looking for something to do."

Joe stopped hiking and turned to face Randy again. He dropped his backpack from his shoulders, unzipped the side pocket, and pulled out a bottle of water. Joe swigged a few gulps while he considered what Randy had suggested. He knew he was the restless type and needed to stay busy, but he had always assumed after retirement he and Fran would be traveling or enjoying something together. He hadn't considered what retired life would be like now.

"I do like to stay busy, Randy," Joe admitted. "And I usually start getting a bit antsy near the end of a vacation. I thought it was because I knew I would be returning to work soon but perhaps it's simply my nature."

"What if we updated your financial projections and assumed you worked until you were seventy or even seventy-five?" Randy offered.

"Seventy or seventy-five?! Are you serious? I'm not sure I want to work that long."

"Have you thought about maybe working part-time instead of full-time at some point? That might be the best of both worlds."

"Honestly, I haven't. My job is pretty demanding, and I don't know too many top-notch attorneys who are working part-time in their seventies."

"Who said you had to be working as an attorney? I know plenty of attorneys who work other jobs."

"I don't know about that. All I've ever been is a lawyer, and I'm too old to learn a new job. That sounds a bit overwhelming."

"Let's take things one step at a time. All I'm suggesting is you could choose to scale back at work, possibly earn a little less, and take more time building better relationships or just doing something for yourself. Because your life would be more balanced and aligned, you might feel less tired and overwhelmed and want to work into your seventies."

Randy and Joe spotted a picnic table in a small clearing overlooking the adjacent valley below. Orange, yellow, and red hues intermingled with the evergreens as the tree line cascaded down the mountain, ending on the embankment of a small pond. The midmorning sun was finally chasing away the gentle morning frost. The landing offered a perfect place to shed a layer of clothing and grab a quick snack.

"How 'bout a break?" Randy asked.

"Sounds good to me," Joe replied. "Not a bad spot, huh?"

"Not at all."

Randy and Joe laid their packs on top of the picnic table and located their snacks and water bottles. They sat in silence for a few moments just enjoying the serenity and beauty of the mountain. Joe was impressed by both the grandness and the simplicity of it all. The outdoors made him happy, and it hadn't cost a thing except for his time. Perhaps this was the lifestyle adjustment Randy was suggesting.

"Hey, Joe," Randy said, "can I show you something?"

"Sure," Joe replied. "Is it another diagram or deck of cards?"

"You know me too well," Randy answered with a smile.

"Really? I was only kidding."

Randy reached into one of the compartments of his backpack and pulled out a deck of cards secured with a rubber band.

"Do you take this stuff with you everywhere you go?" Joe asked, amazed.

"I use this backpack for a lot of things," Randy replied, "but I guess I do. This stuff comes in handy with many of my clients when we're talking about wealth and happiness. But I also keep it with me because it has made a huge difference in my life. It wasn't that long ago when I was going through similar struggles."

"So you carry these cards with you as a reminder?"

"For that, and to show others how important priorities, balance, and happiness are. Understanding the true nature of wealth has changed my life, and I guess it's made me a little evangelical about it."

"I'm impressed, Rabbi Randy."

"Good. Now that I have your full attention, I want to talk to you about engagement."

"Hey, I'm not divorced just yet, and you're not really my type…no offense."

"Very funny, Joe. That's not the kind of engagement I'm talking about."

"Then what are you talking about?"

"The engagement I'm talking about is one of the three major elements of happiness. It refers to being fully engaged, or immersed, in an activity."

"I have some of those experiences."

"But are you having enough of them? Engagement is a critical piece of happiness. It allows us to use our Signature Talents™ for both personal growth and personal achievement."

"Signature Talents™? What are those?"

"Those are talents specific to you that you do really well and make you feel alive. Using your Signature Talents™ is the easiest path to creating more engagement in your life."

"What exactly is engagement?"

"You've heard athletes say they are in the zone, right?"

"Sure. I remember Michael Jordan years ago in the NBA playoffs when he was untouchable. It was amazing."

"That's what it's like to be fully engaged. Hours seem like minutes when we are truly engaged in our lives. It's what the academics call a flow experience, where everything just flows the way it is supposed to. Flow experiences occur when we are engaged in a high-challenge and high-skill activity, and time just seems to stop."

"I've had moments like that at work. When I'm negotiating a deal or helping a client with a strategy, I lose track of time completely. I look up and realize it is much later than I thought."

"Exactly. How often do you have those experiences?"

"Gosh, I don't know. Maybe a few times a week."

"So, if you start to consider another job or career, you would want to make sure it offered you opportunities for plenty of moments like that."

"I'm not really looking to change jobs, Randy. Although I must admit some days it seems like I should. Maybe that would help me get out of this rut. How do you know if something new is going to give you more…what did you call them…flow experiences?"

"The truth is almost any job or activity can be turned into a flow experience if it is a high-challenge and high-skill activity. The easiest way to create engagement, or flow, is to use your Signature Talents™."

"There's that phrase again. Give me a better definition of that."

"Your Signature Talents™ are things that you do exceptionally well, or better than almost anyone else you know. Mine include the ability to create and design processes, form meaningful relationships, and focus on the big picture. What about you?"

"I haven't really thought about it."

"All right, that's what this deck of cards is for," Randy said as he handed Joe the deck.

Joe squared himself at the picnic table and pushed his backpack to the side.

"Joe, I want you to sort the cards into three piles: things you love to do, things you like to do, and things you don't like to do. Once you've chosen the things you love, pick out your top six," Randy instructed.

"I am not clear what things I love to do have to do with my special talents."

"Our Signature Talents™ are most often the things we truly enjoy doing the most. It's the activities during which we tend to lose track of time because we are so immersed in what we are doing."

Joe took several minutes studying the cards and thoughtfully considered each one. He spent a little more time on some than others, but soon he had narrowed his selection to six cards.

"Okay, here are my top six," Joe stated.

Randy took a look at Joe's choices and laid the cards in front of both of them on the picnic table. The cards read as follows:

1. Building Relationships
2. Creating Trust
3. Seeing the Big Picture
4. Putting the Pieces Together
5. Negotiating
6. Making Deals

"They all sound like you. Can you explain what each one means to you personally?" Randy asked.

"Well, they're pretty self-explanatory, but I tend to see them in pairs in terms of my talents. When I thought about my talents and stuff I love to do, I thought about the things that make me successful at work."

"And being successful makes you happy?"

"Absolutely."

"All right, tell me what these six mean to you."

"Well, I am very good at building trust not only with my clients but also with other attorneys…even opposing counsel. And I use trust to build relationships. Relationships are critical for me to do a job well, and both of these things usually come easy for me."

"Very good. What about the others?"

"My clients always compliment me on being able to see the big picture. Honestly, this has always been a strong suit of mine. I appreciate the details, but I don't get bogged down in them. When push comes to shove, I am able to take all the little pieces and put them together so objectives are reached."

"I understand. And the last two talents?"

"I love negotiating, and without meaning to sound cocky, I'm pretty good at it. I have a knack for understanding needs and then leveraging that towards not only the benefit of my clients but towards everyone's benefit. Once I figure that out, I can usually close the deal if a deal is at all possible. That's why clients tend to stick with me because I can negotiate well and close the deal."

"Great. As well as I know you, these make perfect sense to me. I think you have a real good idea of what your Signature Talents™ are. They're not only the things you do well but also the things you thoroughly love to do. Before we put this deck away, I'm going to write them down on this notepad."

Joe took another swig of water while Randy wrote the Signature Talents™ down the middle of the page in a notepad he had in his backpack. A couple of other hikers passed by them along the trial, and Joe waved to them as they walked past, exchanging smiles. The quietness of the mountain had been so pervasive and the conversation so intriguing that Joe was almost startled when the couple suddenly appeared.

"All right, now I have a second deck of cards for you, Joe," Randy stated, putting the first deck away.

"Are you kidding me?" Joe said with a half-grin. "I thought we were hiking today, not playing card games."

"Hey, with me you never know what you might get," Randy replied.

"That's for sure."

Randy pulled a second deck of cards from his backpack, which looked about as weathered as the other but a little thicker.

"This deck contains fifty cards pertaining to work values," Randy stated.

"Work values. What exactly do you mean?" Joe asked.

"Every business has its own work values or culture. None of us works in the perfect environment. Identifying your top work values helps you figure out which business or job is a good fit for you."

"Can you give me an example of some work values?"

"Sure. For me, I love creating and learning. I also like coaching, teaching, and being a visionary, but I don't like managing tasks or people. Therefore, I value a work environment that allows me to do these things without too many managerial responsibilities. At the same time, I know life is more than just work, so I don't want a work environment that requires fifty to sixty hours of my time every week. I need to be able to take vacations and have a flexible schedule."

"I understand. Can I just adopt your work values?"

"Very funny. Just as you have your own unique Signature Talents™, you also have specific work values. You want to work in an environment consistent with your most important values. Otherwise, you'll become frustrated and won't be able to focus on the activities that create flow or engagement."

"So this deck will help me figure that out, I suppose."

"You attorneys are sure bright," Randy said, grinning as he handed Joe the deck. "Go through the cards and pick your top eight work values."

Randy stood and walked toward the edge of the clearing as Joe concentrated on the work value cards. Thick brush separated Randy from the steepest part of the slope, but he was able to peer down far enough to see a young deer several yards below nibbling on some leaves. He considered interrupting Joe but then thought better of it. As he brought a granola bar toward his mouth, the subtle movement alerted the deer to his presence, and it quickly darted away. Randy was amazed at how in tune the deer had been with his surroundings to have been able to see such a tiny movement from so far away.

"Okay," Joe finally said. "Here are my eight cards."

Randy returned to the picnic table and examined Joe's selections. The cards included the following:

1. Integrity
2. Work-Life Balance
3. Intellectual Challenge
4. High Income Potential
5. Independence
6. Decision-Making Opportunity
7. Opportunity to Influence People
8. Chance to Help Others

"You know, Joe," Randy said thoughtfully, "all of these sound very much like you except one: work-life balance."

"Yeah, I know. That's the one most important to me these days," Joe replied. "You know, I've been paying attention to what you've said the last several months."

"Wow, I'm flattered," Randy answered. "So now I have another question for you. How do you see combining work-life balance with high income potential?"

"I don't have to earn what I am currently earning, but I don't want to work for peanuts. I want to have the ability to earn a six-figure income but still have time to enjoy some personal time."

"I see. And what does independence mean to you?"

"Independence to me means being able to choose when I work and how I get the work done. I don't mind being held accountable for results, but I would like to do things my own way."

"I like your list, Joe. I think it suits you," Randy said with a smile.

Randy wrote down Joe's work values along the right side of the page in a column next to his Signature Talents™ as Joe looked on.

"Joe, do you still have your list of life priorities in your wallet?" Randy asked.

"As a matter of fact, I do. Why?"

"Can I see it for a moment?"

"Sure."

Randy took the list from Joe and added his life priorities to the left side of the page on which he had been writing. Joe patiently waited while trying to twist his head around so he could get a better glimpse of the page. After Randy had finished, he turned the notepad around so Joe could clearly see it. It read as follows:

Seeking Balance Worksheet

Life Priorities	Talents	Work Values
1. Loving Parent	1. Relationship-Builder	1. Integrity
2. Health	2. Creating Trust	2. Work–Life Balance
3. Comfortable Life	3. Seeing Big Picture	3. Intellectual Challenge
4. Significant Other	4. Putting Pieces Together	4. High Income Potential
5. Sexuality	5. Negotiating	5. Independence
6. Financial Independence	6. Making Deals	6. Making Decisions
7. Growing and Learning		7. Influencing People
8. Connected to Siblings		8. Helping Others
9. Having Close Friends		
10. Fewer Commitments/Greater Freedom		

"What do you think about it?" Randy asked Joe as he examined the lists.

"About what?" Joe replied, scratching his head. "I'm not sure what I'm supposed to do with these lists side by side. I understand what they represent, but what's the purpose of listing them beside each other?"

"That's a fair question. On the left side, you see your life priorities. Those are the things you value most, right?"

"Right."

"The next column is your Signature Talents™. This is what you do best, and these talents are the best way to create engagement."

"Okay."

"Finally, the third column lists the work values you seek in a job environment."

"Okay, that makes sense."

"When you think about where you want to work, you need to ask yourself if the job reflects your life priorities, allows you to use your Signature Talents™, and has a culture that fits your work values. The right opportunity will match all three. When you find it, you'll have ample opportunities to create lots of engagement or flow experiences."

"And being engaged is one of the three elements to true happiness."

"You've got it! When we're engaged in life, we are realizing our full potential. When that happens, happiness comes naturally. Making connections with others and making a difference in life are the other two keys to happiness."

Joe picked up the notepad and examined the columns on the Seeking Balance worksheet as if he were studying a legal contract. Across the top, Randy had written the three elements of true happiness: connecting with people, engagement in life activities, and making a difference. In the meantime, Randy stood and unzipped a smaller compartment of his backpack, removing some lip balm, which he patiently applied to his lips. The birds chirping overhead and a gentle rustling of the leaves were now easily heard as Joe continued to study the lists. Randy wasn't sure, but it seemed something had really gotten Joe's attention this time.

"Joe, are you okay?" Randy asked after a couple of minutes of silence.

"I'm fine," Joe replied. "I'm just looking to see where my current career fails to measure up."

"What did you come up with?"

"Well, I think my current work environment limits me in two ways. First, it hasn't really allowed me a good work-life balance because of the demands to produce all the time. Second, it probably doesn't allow me the level of independence I would like. I always have to answer to somebody about my production."

"I see. So how is that keeping you from being happy?"

"Well, I don't think it keeps me from using my Signature Talents™ in general, but I do think it hinders me from living my life priorities. My Signature Talents™ fit my job. The problem is my job doesn't fit what I want in my life."

"Like what?"

"Well, I don't read and travel as much as I would like, so growing and learning outside of work is limited. I also haven't been spending enough time on the relationships in my life. And even though I'm healthy now, I don't spend much time exercising. I can't remember the last time I went hiking. More to the point, the concept of greater freedom and fewer commitments is a joke at my firm."

"You're a quick study, Joe. I'm sure your job now has many satisfying aspects, but at the same time it's limiting you."

"I am beginning to understand what you mean."

"So here's the million-dollar question. Is there a place you could work and get more of what you love and less of what you don't like?"

"Honestly, I don't know. I've not given it any thought before this morning."

"I understand, but pause for a moment and think about where you might start if you were considering a new career."

"I suppose I could see a career coach."

"That's a reasonable option. What else?"

"I really don't know. I've been at the same firm for twenty-five years. I can't imagine looking elsewhere."

"But fortunately you've realized you have other options. There might be another job or career that better fits your talents and life priorities."

"Yeah, but it still seems overwhelming."

"It is a huge step. But remember, the issue is almost never that the problem is too big. The issue is usually that we don't have enough support. And where do we get support?"

"From our resources."

"Okay, I'm impressed. You have been listening. Money, time, talents, body and mind, wisdom, and your network provide you with the support you need to tackle almost all problems in life."

"All right, I'll give it some thought. But for now, do you think we could get back to hiking? I feel like I'm in a lecture in the middle of the woods."

"I suppose that's enough for today," Randy said smiling. "Class dismissed."

Both Randy and Joe donned their backpacks and proceeded to climb upwards along the blue trail. Joe hiked in silence for a long while, thinking about what they had just discussed. For months it had seemed that doors had been closing all around him, but today he sensed that some were opening. The higher they climbed, the trees surrounding them became less dense, and the sun climbed along with them. With every step, the day became increasingly brighter and the trail a little less blue.

DECEMBER: MAKING CONNECTIONS

"The glory of friendship is not the outstretched hand, nor the kindly smile, nor the joy of companionship; it is the spiritual inspiration that comes to one when he discovers that someone else believes in him and is willing to trust him."
—Ralph Waldo Emerson

Nearly all the leaves had fallen from the canopy of branches covering the neighborhood street. As Joe drove around the corner, he thought how the overcast sky and chilly temperature created an ideal backdrop for watching football indoors. When Randy suggested coming to his home to watch the Falcons play the Bears, it sounded like the perfect Sunday afternoon outing. Dressed in his red Matt Ryan jersey, Joe was ready to kick back with some comfort food and root for the home team. Maybe this would finally be the Falcons' year.

Joe pulled into Randy's driveway, admiring the recently raked lawn. The paleness of the grass along with holiday decorations confirmed winter had indeed arrived. The heat of summer seemed a distant memory on a day like this. Time had a way of pacifying the past almost to a point beyond recollection…almost. On several occasions, Joe had walked up the same sidewalk to Randy's house with Fran by his side, and no matter how much time passed, he didn't think those memories would ever fade completely. After all, Fran had been a large part of his life and would continue to be from the perspective of being parents.

"Hey there, Joe," Randy said with a big smile as he opened the front door. "So glad you could make it. It's a perfect afternoon for watching a game, huh?"

"Are you kidding?" Joe answered, shaking Randy's hand. "I've been looking forward to this all week. I wouldn't have missed it for anything."

"Come on in and make yourself at home. Laura is out of town for the weekend visiting an old friend, and the kids had plans of their own."

"Yeah, Mark and Marcia both made their own plans for the game today, too. Seems like the whole city's buzzing, with the Falcons in the playoffs."

"I know. Ryan's had a great year. I'm hoping they can make a run for the Super Bowl."

"We'll see. Today's the first step in that direction, I suppose."

"Can I get you something to drink?"

"Sure. I'll have whatever you're having."

Joe made his way downstairs to Randy's den while Randy vanished into the kitchen. The pregame was playing on a large flat screen, and the coffee table was covered with an array of goodies. Chips and salsa, chicken fingers, and vegetable trays were among the offerings as well as a small crock of saucy meatballs. Joe sat down on the couch and looked around the room. Pictures of Randy's two children, his wife, his parents, and several of his friends were scattered everywhere. The place certainly felt like a home.

"Here you go, Joe," Randy said, handing Joe an ice-cold beer. "I hope that's what you had in mind."

"Perfect. Thanks," Joe replied. "Quite the spread you have for us. It looks great. Are you expecting more people?"

"Nope, just you and me. Help yourself. Whatever we don't eat, I'm sure the kids will finish off when they get home later."

"If they're like mine, I'm sure they will. I don't know where they put all the food they eat."

"Is Marcia home from school?"

"Yeah. She came home last week. A lot has happened just since she got home."

"Oh, yeah? Like what?"

"Well, Fran and I finally told the kids we were getting a divorce."

"I remember you telling me you were going to wait until she came home. How'd it go?"

"Better than I thought, actually. My expectations were pretty low based on how they reacted when we told them we were separating. Overall, they took the news pretty well."

"Did you tell them individually or together?"

"Together. I went over to the house after dinner on Wednesday. Fran and I planned it that way. Marcia and Mark knew I was coming, and I'm sure they expected what was coming. Just the fact we called a family meeting probably alerted them to the news."

"Probably so. How did you tell them?"

"I began by telling them Fran and I had decided to divorce. I explained it had nothing to do with them and more to do with Fran and me growing in different directions. Then I told them that we loved them and always would."

"Did Fran say anything?"

"She pretty much repeated what I had said, but she added that she and I would always be their parents and do the best we could for them."

"That sounds encouraging."

"I thought so, too. She's not really talked about us as parents in a while."

"How did the kids take it?"

"Marcia was the first to speak up. She took me off guard because she accused Fran of not trying to fix the marriage. Marcia said she knew about Fran's new boyfriend and that he was the reason marriage counseling hadn't helped."

"Really? Last time she got upset with you, accusing you of working all the time."

"I know. What's weird is I agreed a little with what Marcia was saying, but at the same time I felt protective of Fran. I looked over at Fran and saw her eyes begin to water. I immediately wanted to protect her. I knew I played a big role in our failed marriage and didn't feel right letting her take the fall. The next thing I knew I was coming to her defense."

"What did you say?"

"I told the kids that both of us had made mistakes along the way and that we both had tried to make things work. Unfortunately, it was just too late and we had grown too far apart. I think the fact I spoke up for Fran helped because the kids saw us acting more as a team. I think that helped them realize we would always be together as parents."

"What about Mark?"

"As usual, Mark let Marcia speak first. She is more reactive while Mark is more contemplative. After I had stopped talking, Mark asked if there was any chance we might still get back together. His voice cracked, and I could see tears in his eyes as he asked the question. Honestly, his reaction was tougher to handle than Marcia's accusations."

"That is tough."

"Before I knew it, we were all crying. Randy, I haven't cried in front of my kids in a long, long time. It was a very sad moment. I think we all realized our family would change forever. But at the same time, it seemed like our family was healing in a way. Just sharing the pain together seemed healthy."

"It sounds difficult, but I agree it also sounds very healthy."

"After a few moments, I pulled myself together. I told them this was a big change, and it would take time to adjust. But if they had any questions, they could ask Fran or me."

"I would say you handled that really well, Joe. In fact, both of you handled that pretty well. That must make you feel good."

"I don't know if that's possible, but it went okay. Mark then offered to go to an in-state college because he said he knew divorces were expensive. I almost teared up all over again."

"What did you say?"

"I found myself saying the same things you've been telling me. I told them I made a good living and that they both could continue with their plans for school and college. I told them Fran and I would always work hard to give them the support they needed, and that we would always love them."

"I've been a good influence on you," Randy said with a grin.

"I suppose you have," Joe admitted. "After that, I told them I'd been doing a lot of thinking over the last few months and that I hadn't been spending my time the way I would like. I told them I was committed to making time for the really important things in life."

"That's wonderful. I'm sure they loved hearing that."

"I don't know if they did or not. I'm not usually emotional with them, but the moment brought it out of me and it felt very natural."

"That's a good thing, Joe. It's important to show your kids a person can learn and grow from life's challenges. Knowing that anyone at any time can redirect their life according to the things they most value is an important lesson to learn."

"I just wished I had learned it earlier."

"I understand, but the sad fact is sometimes pain is the sledgehammer that helps us break our old destructive patterns and creates the freedom to move to a happier and healthier life. We all experience pain in our lives. Some of us take the opportunity to reflect and grow from the experience while others blame situations and people for their misfortune. Be thankful you are among the former."

Joe raised his beer, and Randy joined him as they both took a swig. The game was getting ready to start, and the announcers struggled to speak above the crowd in the Georgia Dome. With Randy's encouragement, Joe put a sampling of food on a plate and began to eat. Both of them focused their attention toward the screen as the opening kickoff ensued. Joe had forgotten how much he enjoyed Sunday afternoon football at a friend's house, and he smiled in contentment as he took a moment to appreciate Randy's hospitality. Randy had been much more than a financial advisor and casual acquaintance. He had become a close and valued friend.

"You know, Randy," Joe began, "I really did a lot of thinking after our hike last month."

"Oh, yeah?" Randy replied, looking away from the television. "Did we jar something loose?"

"Very funny. I guess after seeing my life priorities, talents, and work values all side by side, I started wondering if there might be a better place for me."

"You mean a better place to work?"

"Yeah. I ended up showing my Seeking Balance worksheet to a few people, and their reactions were surprising."

"Who did you show it to?"

"The first person I showed it to was a friend of mine who works for a boutique investment bank. After looking it over, he asked if I'd be interested in joining his team."

"Really? What do you think?"

"I was pretty shocked, honestly. First of all, accounting is not my strong suit, and secondly I wasn't really looking to make a change just yet."

"He must have seen something he liked."

"I guess so. I told him I wasn't good at accounting, but he told me they were looking for someone to engender trust, build relationships, and seal the deal. He thought I would be perfect for that. He said they could always hire a freshly minted MBA to run the numbers."

"What do you think?"

"The offer has some appeal in that investment bankers make good money, and I do like deal-making. But I'm not so sure it offers the work-life balance I'm looking for. When a deal gets hot, investment bankers typically drop everything to chase it."

"So you'd be concerned about not having enough time off?"

"I'd be more concerned about not having control of my time. I want to have more time for myself. I want to make new friends and spend more time with my family."

"I'm impressed. That doesn't even sound like the old Joe. It seems to me you now realize that time, not money, is your real limiting resource, and you're committed to spending time on what matters most to you. That's a very hard lesson for many people to internalize."

"You're right! Oh my gosh, what have you done to me, Randy?" Joe asked teasingly.

"All part of the master plan, Joe," Randy replied. "How about another beer?"

"Sounds good."

Randy stepped out of the room just in time to avoid seeing the Bears score their first touchdown. Joe watched the replay, which showed a breakdown in communication in Atlanta's secondary, leaving one of the Bears' receivers wide open for the score. The first quarter was almost over, and the Bears had drawn first blood.

"The Bears scored I see," Randy said, handing Joe a beer on his return. "What happened?"

"Breakdown in communication. The Bears receiver was all by himself in the end zone," Joe replied.

"True in football and true in life. So many problems happen because of poor communication."

"I was thinking the same thing."

"So, did you share your worksheet with anyone else?"

"Actually, I did. I had a routine appointment with my divorce attorney, Martin Egleston. As an attorney, I thought he would be able to relate to my situation better than others."

"What did he say?"

"Without my even asking, he pretty much offered me a job as well. Martin is part of a full-service firm. Here I am thinking I'm too old and too entrenched in my job to make a change, and within a couple of weeks and without really making an effort, I receive two job offers."

"I'm not surprised. You're a talented lawyer with a loyal client base that consistently generates significant billings. Lots of firms would love to have you on their team."

"I guess so. Anyway, after talking with him, it sounds like there are some good things and some bad things with his offer."

"Such as?"

"Well, they don't have the production requirements at their firm, and they don't have any associates. But on the down side, their billing rates are about forty percent less than at my current firm."

"Ouch. That's a pretty big difference. What are your thoughts?"

"I love the idea of no production requirements. If I want to work less, nobody's going to give me grief. But having associates is both good and bad. On the one hand, I like teaching and mentoring an associate, and I enjoy being able to delegate the rudimentary work to someone else. But on the other hand, many clients don't want associates working on their files, and the associates' billings are often an issue."

"I understand."

"In addition, the lower billable rates are a challenge. My clients would love it, but I'm not sure I want to leave that much money on the table."

"What does that mean in terms of take-home salary?"

"I'm not sure. They don't have as much overhead as my current firm, so it may not be much of a cut. But with lower billing rates, my work volume could soar, which would mean even less time with family and friends. I don't have all the details and, honestly, I haven't thought much about it. It all took me by surprise."

"Does Egleston's firm match up with your work values, priorities, and talents?"

"I would have to say they match up pretty well. I would have the independence I wanted, and if I could manage my work flow, I would have the ability to have a good work-life balance. At the same time, I would still be negotiating, making deals, and building relationships. I don't know if I would earn enough to have a comfortable lifestyle, though."

"So assuming the income part works out, his firm might offer you a greater chance to become engaged and have more frequent flow experiences?"

"I guess it would as long as I didn't get stuck doing too much basic boring work. It certainly gives me something to think about."

"You know, Joe, it just goes to show how powerful your network is and the opportunities that arise when you share with people who you are and what you want in life."

"You're right. If I had never shared my priorities, values, and talents with Martin or Tom, I would have never known these opportunities existed."

"Not only did the conversations create new opportunities, but they also helped you clarify what you want in your next job. Your discussion with Martin has made you think about whether or not you want associates."

"That's true."

"You know, Joe, I don't want to sound too preachy, but I've learned from personal experience how important good friends can be."

"Yeah, I guess that is an area I've neglected for a long time."

"I did, too, during my first marriage. I didn't really invest much time and energy into the close relationships I had."

"Fortunately, I still have some good friends like you and Martin."

"When you think about it, you have a great relationship with Martin. You trust him and you know he cares about you. My hunch is you don't worry about Martin judging you. Right?"

"Absolutely. Martin is a great guy. He's comfortable in his own skin and very non-judgmental."

"Because he doesn't judge you, you were able to tell him what you want. As you self-disclosed, you self-discovered and created a clearer picture of what you really wanted."

"I hadn't thought about it in those terms, but I guess that's true. Plus, it is just nice to know you have options. I no longer feel forced to stay where I am."

"Exactly."

"I guess Martin is a really great friend," Joe stated.

"I have found it takes three things to have a really great relationship. The first is mutual trust. You trust the other person to tell you the truth and never throw you under the bus."

"Okay."

"The second is mutual caring. When times are tough, close friends are there for each other."

"Definitely."

"And third, and maybe the most important, is the ability to talk to the other person without a fear of judgment. We self-discover as we self-disclose, and we only disclose to someone we trust, who cares for us, and who doesn't judge us."

"Randy, you fit all three of those criteria for me. You probably know as much about me as anyone now."

"I'm honored, Joe. I appreciate you having that kind of trust in me."

"But you go beyond that."

"What do you mean?"

"You follow up on me to be sure I do what I say I'll do," Joe answered with a warm smile.

"Oh, that," Randy said, also smiling. "That's called accountability. What are friends for if they can't help you see your own blind spots?"

"I just wish I didn't have so many!"

Joe and Randy took a moment to enjoy some snacks and watch the next series of plays as Matt Ryan led the Falcons methodically down the field. They scored the tying touchdown just as the first half ended. Highlights of Atlanta's football season appeared on the screen, grabbing Randy and Joe's attention away from the conversation. Without a word, both of them admired many of the spectacular moments, feeling a sense of pride.

Then immediately following the segment, the NFL's United Way promotion showed the hundreds of children and families who had been helped throughout the greater Atlanta area. The images naturally made Joe think about Helping Hands.

"Speaking of connections and support, I forgot to tell you I went back to Helping Hands last week," Joe stated.

"Really? With Mark?" Randy replied.

"No, this time I went by myself. I had such a good experience before that I decided to go to Helping Hands yesterday to help out."

"That's great, Joe."

"Not much was going on at the center, so Bruce Shaw and I just cleaned up a bit."

"Bruce is the director, right?"

"Right. We talked most of the afternoon, and he's a pretty inspiring person."

"Tell me."

"As it turns out, Bruce used to be a vice president in the sales and marketing department at G.E. Most of his time was consumed with traveling and chasing the deal. He was very successful but also extremely busy."

"So how did he become the director at Helping Hands?"

"To make a long story short, his boss at G.E. offered him an early retirement package when Bruce was forty-five. Bruce wasn't really interested because he still had visions of climbing the corporate ladder, but his boss told him it was in his best interest to take the deal because lay-offs were coming."

"Nothing like having the rug pulled out from under you."

"I know. Bruce was pretty pissed, but after talking with his wife, he decided to take six months off and think about what he wanted to do next."

"That seems to make sense to me, and it took a lot of guts."

"I agree," Joe said. "Anyway, he had a lot of the same worries I have now. He didn't know if he and his family could get by without his big corporate income, and he didn't want to change his lifestyle. I completely related to him."

"I can see why."

"Despite his worries, he took off the six months, and that's when he started volunteering at Helping Hands. After three months, the board there asked Bruce to be the executive director, and he said yes."

"Wow. Talk about a change of career."

"I know. He took a big hit in salary, but he says he has never regretted his decision."

"I'm impressed. Did you happen to ask Bruce what prompted him to take the leap?"

"It sounds like Bruce's support and source of strength came from his wife. She made him realize how much happier he had been since volunteering at Helping Hands. He was constantly talking about ways to help the center raise money and telling stories about people he had helped each week. They assessed what sacrifices they would have to make, and, in the end, taking the director's job seemed like the right thing to do."

"Bruce's wife is a smart, courageous lady. She realized he was happy and most engaged when helping others at

Wealth and Happiness

Helping Hands. She must have been willing to take the financial leap of earning less and cutting back. Bruce is lucky to have her."

"Yeah, I guess so."

"What kind of adjustments did they have to make?"

"Bruce said they remortgaged their house to lower the payments and placed their kids in public school instead of private school. He said they hold on to their cars now instead of trading them in every three years, eat out less often and at less expensive restaurants, and travel a little more modestly. He doesn't view any of those adjustments as a big deal."

"And he's happier?"

"Definitely. He feels like he has it all. He talks about being a great fit for his job and having a clear vision for Helping Hands' future. He really cares about the women at the shelter and loves watching them change their lives for the better. They can't help everyone, and they have their share of failures. But, as Bruce says, the success stories are incredibly satisfying."

"That's a great story, Joe. That is inspiring."

"Bruce showed me it's not impossible to change careers late in life. I was really glad I went to Helping Hands and had a conversation with him."

"Do you think you could work for a nonprofit or charity?"

"I don't think that's my thing. I enjoy being an attorney, making deals, and negotiating. But I see changing jobs or careers can offer greater happiness and fulfillment for some people."

"I must say, Joe, you've come a long way," Randy said, giving Joe a pat on the back. "You're talking about the things in life that really matter."

"I'm pretty hard-headed, but I've realized how important my family, my siblings, and friends are to me. I need to make time for these priorities. There might be a better job out there that can give me the things I love professionally and also give me more time to be with those I care about."

"I'm really glad to hear optimism in your voice. Now if you could just spread some of that optimism on to the Falcons. Looks like it's still tied."

"Hey, I'll do my best."

"You'd better. The fourth quarter just started, and we could use a little luck," Randy said, turning up the television volume slightly.

"This is the best part of the game, Randy," Joe replied. "The game is in the balance and anything could happen."

"Right!" Randy replied with a knowing grin. "That's the kind of attitude I like to hear."

JANUARY: MAKING A DIFFERENCE

"Since you get more joy out of giving joy to others, you should put a good deal of thought into the happiness that you are able to give."

—Eleanor Roosevelt

Joe walked briskly across the parking lot. A passerby may have thought his pace was due to the frigid temperatures that had embraced the Southeast over the last several days, but Joe wasn't thinking much about the cold. In fact, he felt pretty warm inside. The morning sunshine seemed to flow right through him as he made his way toward the diner. He hummed a song he had heard on the radio, keeping its beat with his stride. It was going to be a wonderful day.

As usual, Randy was early for breakfast and sat in their usual corner booth of the diner, reading the news. Joe unbundled himself, placing his scarf and coat on an already full coat rack. The diner was bustling with people, and nearly everyone hugged a cup of coffee, trying to keep their hands warm. Joe signaled to the waitress for a cup as well as he walked to join his dear friend for their monthly morning ritual.

"What's going on in the world today?" Joe asked, interrupting Randy in the middle of an article.

"Hey there, Joe," Randy replied. "Nothing earth-shattering, thank goodness. The market finally looks to be settling down a bit."

"That's good to hear. I guess I don't have to beat you up over shrinking stock values then," Joe said with a smile.

"Not today anyway. You sure are in a good mood. Did you have a great date last night or meet someone new?"

"No, but I have been feeling pretty good lately. For once I feel like I have some control over the changes in my life, and it feels nice."

"Oh, yeah? I can't wait to hear all about this."

"Let me at least get a cup of coffee first. I'd hate to leave out any of the details, you know."

As if on cue, the waitress placed a piping-hot cup of coffee in front of Joe along with a handful of creamers. Joe nodded and smiled at her and proceeded to stir cream into his coffee. In the meantime, Randy took a sip of his own coffee and patiently waited for Joe, who seemed to be leisurely taking his time.

"Okay, anytime today," Randy said after Joe had stirred his coffee for nearly a minute.

"Nothing like a captive audience," Joe replied. "I wanted to be sure I had your complete attention."

"When have you not had my complete attention?"

"Good point. I must say you have listened to plenty of my stories these last several months that have been less than interesting."

"That's not true. It's all been interesting, and you've come a long way in a short time."

"Well, in that spirit, I'll tell you what's happened since I last saw you. You remember when I was over at your house last month? I told you two different people had offered me a position with their firms."

"Right, I remember. The other law firm and the investment bankers."

"Well, I went home and thought really hard about making a career change. The law firm and the investment banking firm both had intriguing possibilities, but neither of them seemed just right. At the same time, the fact I was interested at all made it clear to me I wasn't happy in my current situation."

"That makes sense."

"Anyway, I went to work the next morning as usual. I sat down in my office and started my day as I always do. As I began to muddle through stacks of papers on my desk and prepare for appointments later in the day, a letter from Mark's school caught my attention."

"From Mark's school? Was it something bad?"

"No, not at all. It was a notice letting parents know that an awards ceremony was being held at the end of the semester, and Mark was receiving an award for academic excellence."

"That's really great."

"Yes and no. It was great he was getting the award, but not so great it was that afternoon and I had a list of appointments. The note had been on my desk for two weeks, and I simply overlooked it. In the past, Fran would always make sure I knew about these awards and coax me into blocking out my schedule. Even then, I was often too busy to get away."

"So what did you do?"

"I sat back in my chair, and all of a sudden things just clicked. I was faced with making a decision. I could either choose to cancel the afternoon's appointments and go to Mark's awards ceremony or I could convince myself I was too busy to leave the office, like I usually do. I knew what my priorities were, but the question was whether I was going to put my money where my mouth was…so to speak."

Joe took a sip of his coffee, which was now cool enough to swallow, and as he did, the waitress came by prepared to take their breakfast order. She was the same middle-aged woman who had served them many times before, but this time Joe noticed an unusual turquoise ring she wore on her right index finger. It was somewhat oval but irregular in shape, and its lack of a polished finish made it seem more authentic than most turquoise stones he had seen. As they placed their orders, Joe wondered why he had never noticed it previously.

"I'm dying of suspense here. So what did you do?" Randy asked almost pleadingly.

"My secretary and I got on the phone and cancelled all my afternoon appointments," Joe replied with a sense of satisfaction. "Randy, it was the first time I had ever done anything like that."

"I think that's great, Joe. It might sound strange, but I'm proud of you."

"I was proud of myself, actually. And when I walked into the school auditorium and Mark saw me there, words can't describe the look on his face."

"I bet. I take it he was happy to see you there?"

"He was. As I watched him walk across the stage and get his award, I knew it had been the right decision and that no amount of money I would have made at work that afternoon would have been worth it. I made Mark's day, and he made mine."

"That is really great, Joe. By being at the ceremony, you showed Mark how much you care and how proud you are of him. You made a huge deposit into Mark's emotional bank account, and your actions and your life priorities were aligned. It's no surprise it made your day."

"It's true, Randy. I just hate that I've missed out on so many opportunities for these special moments with both my children over the years."

"We all have regrets. It is part of life. But instead of focusing on the lost opportunities, I suggest celebrating on how far you've come over the past year. Your progress is nothing short of amazing."

"That afternoon made me start thinking even more."

"What do you mean? Thinking about what?"

"After the awards ceremony, I went back to the office. I made a few phone calls to clients. As we talked, I realized I really liked my job. I like the people I help. I enjoy the type of work I do. And without sounding cocky, I'm pretty good at it, too."

"I know you're great at it. It's why your clients pay you what they do."

"I really don't want to change jobs or careers. I like what I do. I just want to manage it better and do it a little less."

"But I thought that was the problem. Didn't you tell me your firm's philosophy was built on sixty-hour work weeks? If you fail to meet those standards, won't Seth come down hard on you?"

"That's true. I have always been afraid if I cut back at work, I would be asked to leave and have to work for a less profitable firm. I imagined working just as hard for less money, and that was never appealing. So, I just kept working, a hamster on my hamster wheel."

"So what changed?"

"I realized I have choices. Without even trying, I got two great job offers. I don't have to keep up this pace at work."

"So what did you decide?"

"I always tell my kids you don't get what you want if you don't ask. So I decided to talk with Seth about restructuring my relationship with the firm. "

"It sounds to me like you are moving from fear to confidence."

"What are you talking about?"

"Before, you were scared about what would happen if you cut back at work. Your fear left you feeling like you didn't have any other options, so you just kept trudging along."

"I guess that's true."

"Now, that's all changed. You are in a place of confidence now. You've realized you're a darn good lawyer, and you have several opportunities before you. With your newfound confidence, you're willing to engage Seth in a conversation about what you want. And you are using your Signature Talents™ in the process."

"I guess you're right. I certainly didn't consider talking with Seth about a solution before."

The waitress returned and placed two steaming bowls of oatmeal on the table with brown sugar and raisins on the side as well as a bowl of fresh fruit that Randy had ordered.

"Would you gentlemen care for a refill on your coffees?" she asked.

"Yes, please," Joe replied. "And if you don't mind, could I also get a bowl of fruit?"

"Of course," she said with a smile. "I'll be right back."

"Turning over a new leaf?" Randy asked, noticing Joe hadn't ordered his usual hearty breakfast.

"Maybe I am," Joe answered with teasing defiance. "You got a problem with that?"

"Me? Absolutely not. I'd like you to live a long and healthy life. I need all the clients I can get."

"Very funny."

The waitress returned with Joe's bowl of fruit and refreshed both men's cups with hot coffee. The oatmeal was the perfect breakfast for such a cold morning, and both Randy and Joe enjoyed the warm feeling in their stomachs. Despite the pleasant interruption, Randy's attention was hardly deterred from their conversation.

"So I have to know," Randy said anxiously. "What did Seth say when you spoke to him?"

"Well, I didn't go talk with him that afternoon," Joe admitted. "I'm not even sure I would have made time to see him the next morning. But as luck would have it, he asked to see me."

"Any special reason?"

"Yeah, he wanted to talk about why I had cancelled my appointments the day before on such short notice."

"Wow, he really keeps a tight leash on things."

"Not really, but he had come by my office looking for me and noticed I was gone. After my secretary told him I was out for the afternoon, and with his concerns about my production, he felt we needed to talk. Anyway, I had a message the next morning that he wanted to have lunch with me. I decided it was time to have a conversation about changing my role at the firm."

"Good for you, Joe. That took real courage."

"So lunchtime comes, and I go into Seth's office. He stands up and shakes my hand formally, like he always does, and then he immediately dives right into the heart of the matter. He wants to know what's going on with me and why I cancelled all my appointments."

"Doesn't feel like the warm and fuzzies."

"That's Seth most of the time. He tends to be serious and all-business. But for whatever reason, it didn't seem to faze me that day. I just told him flat out that Mark had an awards ceremony I wanted to attend."

"Nothing like honesty."

"I agree, but I could tell he didn't like my reason for taking off half the day. I know he's under a lot of pressure. He went into this long speech about how the firm really needs to be sensitive to our clients' needs and how production is down compared to prior years. Because my billable hours are a premium source of revenue for the firm, he needs me to put solid hours on the books."

"In other words, he was trying to place the firm's priorities over your own."

"Well said. So I listened patiently until he was finished, and then I began using my negotiation skills on my own behalf for once. I told Seth that my life was changing. I told him I loved my work and the firm, but that I was interested in having a life outside of the firm. My work there was just too consuming, and it was affecting my happiness."

"How did he react?"

"Not too well initially. He said I should consider finding another firm. Because the firm is based on a philosophy of hard-working lawyers providing high-quality legal work, they had never tolerated anyone who wanted to work less than full speed."

"I see."

"But then my creativity and deal-making skills kicked into gear. I reminded him that times were tough and there was a lot of empty office space. I also reminded him several partners were underemployed and looking for additional work."

"So?"

"I told him that if I cut back, other struggling members of the firm like Paul Green or Stacey Bloom could pick up my slack, creating a win-win situation. I've been incredibly busy with Windmill Technologies, and both of these guys are great lawyers looking for extra work. I also made him aware that if I left to join another firm, my clients would most likely go with me."

"I'm sure that got his attention."

"It certainly did."

"Okay, I understand. But what about your other partners? Won't they be resentful?"

"If I continued as a partner, they probably would be resentful. But I told Seth I should resign from the partnership and become of-counsel to the firm. You know, someone who is not necessarily a partner but more of an associate."

"What about your income? How big a hit would you be looking at?"

"I told Seth I wanted my reduction in time and reduction in pay to be proportionate."

"Did he go for it?"

"It took a little persuading, but eventually he did. It just made sense for everyone."

"So what did you finally decide?"

"I told Seth I wanted to work a normal forty-hour week instead of a sixty-hour one," Joe stated. "In doing so, I would take home exactly one-third less income from what I have been making annually the last three years."

"And he was okay with that?"

"He wanted to think it over and play with the numbers, but the numbers must have worked for him because he called me back the next day and said it was a go."

"So basically you used his own complaints about the firm's decreased production to work a deal for yourself?"

"Isn't that what good negotiators do?"

"Now you're sounding a little cocky," Randy said with a grin. "How's that gonna work out for you financially?"

"You're asking me? What do you do for a living?"

"Let me rephrase my question, counselor. I know my perspective on your financial situation, but how do you feel about making two-thirds of the money you were making before?"

"I keep thinking about Bruce Shaw. With both kids in school and a pending divorce, it's not the best time to take a cut in pay. But I will still be earning a nice living, and I'm tired of spending my life at work. If Bruce Shaw can make it on his income, so can I."

"I'm really impressed with you, Joe."

"Thanks. I am finally beginning to understand what you have been telling me all along. Time is my most limited resource. More money is not going to make me happy, but if I spend more time with the people I love, I have a real shot at a better life."

"I couldn't have said it better myself."

"Plus, I've been thinking about what you said last month. I really do like my work. If I don't burn myself out, there's no reason I can't work until I'm at least seventy years old. That takes a lot of pressure off me."

Joe and Randy finished the rest of their breakfast and washed it down with a sip of coffee. Within a couple of minutes, the waitress had returned, collected their empty bowls, and refilled their mugs. No matter how busy the diner became, she always maintained a pleasant attitude and a contagious smile for her customers. She truly seemed to enjoy what she was doing.

"So when does your new schedule begin?" Randy asked.

"It already has. Can't you tell by my relaxed attitude?" Joe replied as he sat back and laid his arm against the back of the booth.

"I must say you do look more content than I've seen you in a long time."

"Randy, I really am happier. Once I made the jump, I haven't looked back. I've even started playing basketball at my gym again."

"Really? I didn't know you liked playing basketball."

"I love it, but it's one of those things I gave up a long time ago, telling myself work wouldn't allow me the time. I feel so much better about myself since I started playing again."

"That explains the choice of breakfast this morning."

"Well, maybe. I guess I am thinking a little more about my diet. Hard to make a jump shot with too many extra pounds."

"What other changes have you made in your life with the extra time?"

"Well, let's see...I'm volunteering twice a month still at Helping Hands. Mark goes with me at least one of those times."

"Really? What exactly are you doing there?"

"Actually, you might say I'm using my Signature Talents™. Bruce needed some help administratively, for one thing. They are looking for a new facility, and so he asked me to be involved in helping negotiate the best deal for them."

"Now that's getting the most out of your skills, Joe."

"That part's great, but honestly I like helping the women there most of all. I've started teaching them interview skills and helping them find jobs that match their talents. I've always been good at putting the pieces together and seeing the big picture. Randy, you would be amazed at the appreciation these women have after we talk about possibilities."

"It's nice to have someone to help you out when things aren't going your way."

"I can certainly relate to that, but I feel so worthwhile by helping them. I believe they do more for me than I do for them."

"That's how making a difference in other people's lives brings us joy and happiness. It's definitely a two-way street."

"I know Mark feels the same way. He looks forward to going, and getting to spend time with him is a bonus for me."

"I know when my kids were teenagers, they always wanted to be with their friends and not necessarily with their dad."

"Mark's the same way, but Helping Hands has been a place he really enjoys going to with me. Come to think of it, maybe I should encourage him to invite one of his friends to come along next time."

"That's a great idea. It's nice to be able to share your happiness with others. There's enough happiness for all of us; it's not one of those things that's a zero-sum game. By the way, how's Marcia doing?"

"Marcia is back at Michigan. She had a really nice break, and with my new schedule, we got to spend some time together. She's a great kid."

"What did she think about your new work schedule?"

"Marcia has always been the more practical one. Even though she can be emotional at times, she gets to the nuts and bolts of a situation pretty quickly. The first thing she wanted to know was how my reduced income would affect things."

"I wonder who she gets that from?" Randy asked with a grin.

"Aren't you a comedian this morning?" Joe replied. "Anyway, once I reassured her things would be fine, she seemed genuinely happy for me."

"I'd say you're setting a good example for her, Joe."

"I hope I am. I'm gonna take some time in March to visit her in Michigan. I haven't done that since her freshman year. It's been way too long."

"Joe, you have really turned the corner. Look how your life has changed in just this one year. You're making time for your kids, renegotiating your relationship with your firm, and actively working to help struggling women get back on their feet. You've come a long way, my friend."

"It's true. I'm also finding I'm not as rushed when I talk on the phone. I can sit and have a conversation with my brother for half an hour without feeling like I'm not fulfilling some obligation."

"You seem like you have more energy, too."

"I think I do. Even though I'm probably doing as much if not more every day, I feel energized. I feel I am more connected to what's going on around me."

"My hunch is you're energized because you've aligned your life with your life priorities, and because you're making a difference in other people's lives. It feels great when we help someone else. You made a difference to Mark when you showed up last week at his awards ceremony, and your work at Helping Hands is clearly making a difference. My guess is you're making a difference in other areas of your life, too."

"I agree," Joe said, nodding. "I still make a difference in my clients' lives, and I am also making a difference in the lives of my family and friends because I'm more involved in their lives. It felt great helping my brother last month with some issues he was dealing with at work."

"Making a difference makes us feel more connected and alive. It's no wonder you feel you have more energy. I am sure your clients will notice the change as well."

Joe finished off the last of his coffee and looked around the diner. Fewer tables were now occupied as people had left to start their day. Everyone was busy, and everyone was focused on a schedule. Joe was no different, but what was different was his level of engagement in the life around him. Over the last several months, he had figured out his true priorities, his talents, and the difference between happiness and pleasure. And by realigning his life with these priorities, he was happier than he had been in a long time. Despite all the negatives over the past several months, he was beginning to see a huge ray of sunshine enter his life.

The waitress made her way back to Randy and Joe's table and offered coffee refills once again. After both of them declined, she placed their check on the table.

"You gentlemen take care of that whenever you're ready," she said with a smile and a glance at each of them. "No rush."

"Excuse me, do you mind if I ask where you got that ring?" Joe asked, pointing to her right hand.

"Not at all," she replied. "I bought it when I was in New Mexico a few years ago."

"Really?" Joe said. "It's unique. I like the fact it's not as polished and symmetric as most turquoise rings you see."

"Me, too. It's a little beat-up, like me," the waitress replied, letting out a slight chuckle.

"Well, I don't know about that, but I would say you have excellent taste," Joe commented.

"Thank you," she said with a gracious smile. "You gentlemen have a very nice day."

The waitress moved on to the next table with a slight bounce in her step while Joe and Randy settled their portion of the check. Then they both began to bundle up for the cold.

"You know, Joe," Randy said, "I think you made our waitress' morning."

"I had been admiring her ring all morning," Joe replied. "I meant it. She does have nice taste."

"Still, it's one thing to think it and another thing to say it."

"You know, I probably wouldn't have noticed her ring a year ago. I was too preoccupied with things that just didn't matter all that much. But now, I seem to focus in on little things like that."

"You're definitely more engaged and, if I do say so, happier. It's great to see."

"And you're a big reason I'm where I am," Joe said, softly slapping Randy on the shoulder.

"Now you've made my morning, too," Randy replied with a grin.

Randy and Joe walked out together and headed to their cars. The frigid air felt bitter on their faces and sent a shiver through their bodies. But despite the chill, the sun continued to shine brilliantly. It was definitely going to be a good day.

MAY (FOUR MONTHS LATER): AN ANNIVERSARY CELEBRATION

"The more you praise and celebrate your life, the more there is in life to celebrate."

—Oprah Winfrey

The parking lot was full, but Joe had a good feeling. He bypassed several rows of cars and drove all the way to the front. As luck would have it, a car was just pulling out of a space only a few steps from the restaurant door. Joe patiently waited as he smiled over his good fortune. Mickey's was packed tonight, and Joe was thankful he had made reservations in advance. But as he pulled into the parking space, he wasn't thinking about crowds and reservations. In fact, he wasn't necessarily thinking about steak.

As Joe entered the lobby of the restaurant, he spotted Randy seated at the dark mahogany bar over to the right, having a conversation with the bartender. Small reading lamps peppered the bar top, giving it the appearance of a law library of sorts. And the tiered array of high-end bourbons and scotches behind the bar assured even the most discerning patron his or her thirst could be quenched. As for Randy, he was having a glass of red wine, and Joe thought that looked like just the thing.

"How are you, Randy?" Joe asked, extending his hand toward his friend. "The place is a little more crowded than the last time we were here, huh?"

"Joe, great to see you!" Randy said, rising from his bar stool to shake Joe's hand. "How have you been? I know it's only been a few months since I've seen you, but it feels like a year."

"Yeah, you miss a couple of months in my life, it may as well be a year," Joe said with a grin.

"May I offer you a cocktail, sir?" The bartender asked Joe.

"Sure. What are you having, Randy?"

"A pinot noir."

"All right, sounds good. Thanks."

Joe took one of the few vacant seats next to Randy at the bar, and the bartender placed a cocktail napkin in front of him. Several people stood, holding their cocktails as they waited for their tables to be readied, and the buzz of conversation made for a festive atmosphere.

"So, what's the occasion? Don't get me wrong. I'm glad you invited me out for steak on a Saturday night instead of our usual breakfast meetings, but I didn't know if you had something big to tell me," Randy said.

"Well, I don't have anything earth-shattering to tell you, but it has been a full year since Fran dropped the bomb on me," Joe replied.

"Absolutely. A lot has happened since then."

"That's an understatement."

"But look at you!" Randy said, appraising his friend. "You look great, and you seem happy."

"And I owe a lot of that to you, Randy. That's why I wanted to take you to Mickey's tonight…my treat."

"Joe, you know that's not necessary."

"Randy, certain things in life are more important than money. Tonight is my treat to thank you for all of your help and support over the last year. It hasn't been easy, but I'm in a better place."

The hostess called Joe's name for his table just as the bartender delivered his glass of wine. Joe made the necessary arrangements at the bar, and Randy and Joe followed the hostess to a table adjacent to a large picture window overlooking a small outdoor courtyard. In the center of the courtyard, a ceramic fountain bubbled amidst lavish botanicals. It was so peaceful and serene, and Joe felt much the same way inside. He chuckled to himself as he remembered how un-peaceful he had been the same time last year.

The hostess placed a wine list on the table and informed them the waiter would be with them shortly as both Randy and Joe admired their surroundings.

"So, how have things been with you?" Joe asked, turning to Randy.

"Things are good," Randy replied. "I've got some technology challenges at work, but nothing insurmountable. I just got back from a trip to Rome and Florence with the family. We hired a private guide in each city, and it was money well spent. It's amazing how much more you can see in a day with a great guide."

"That sounds fun. I'm planning on going to Italy in July. You'll have to tell me some of your favorite places so I can try them."

"I'd be happy to. Who are you going with?"

"I'm taking Mark and Marcia with me for a week. They're pretty excited about it, actually."

"Who wouldn't be?"

"Well, some kids their ages don't necessarily want to go to Europe with their dad. But I'm glad they're looking forward to it. I'm so much closer to them now than I was a year ago."

"That's a tribute to you. You made the decision to be open and honest with them and to spend more time with them. You chose to help Mark at Helping Hands, and you never badmouthed Fran in front of the kids."

"I still feel disappointed I didn't spend more time with them sooner, but better late than never. I went to see Marcia at Michigan last month, and I'm helping Mark move into his dorm in August. He got accepted to Purdue."

"Purdue! Tell him congratulations. That's great."

"Yeah, he was happy because it was his first choice. I'm really proud of both of them. Despite all the changes in their lives this past year, they've weathered it really well. Marcia made the dean's list again despite it all."

"You've been a great dad, Joe. Despite the chaos of your life, you continued to support your kids and be there for them, knowing they had never wished any of this on themselves."

"Excuse me, gentlemen," the waiter said, interrupting their conversation. "May I offer you another glass of wine or something different?"

"I'm fine," Randy said.

"I'm fine, too, for now, but can we get a bottle of the Founders' Estate Cabernet with dinner?" Joe requested.

"Of course. Would you like to hear this evening's specials?" the waiter continued.

The waiter listed a variety of entrées, all of which sounded delicious. Joe listened intently, noticing the dedication this young waiter had given to memorizing the different menu options. He presented each with appealing details and appeared passionate about the food. It was quite admirable. Each item sounded more exquisite than the preceding one, and Joe couldn't decide which sounded the best.

"Let me ask you," Joe said to the waiter. "What would you recommend?"

"From the specials, the porterhouse with cabernet demi-glaze and the strawberry vinaigrette salad is really delicious. But you can never go wrong with our prime rib either," the waiter said.

"I'll have the porterhouse and strawberry vinaigrette then."

The waiter took Randy's order and left Joe and Randy enjoying their wine and gazing into the outdoor courtyard. Joe thought about Fran for a moment and what she might be doing on a Saturday evening. Was she on a date or just sitting at home watching TV? It didn't matter, but Joe wondered all the same. He still cared about her despite all the ups and downs they had experienced over the year.

"Have you talked to Fran lately?" Randy asked.

"Not in a few weeks," Joe replied. "The divorce was finalized in March, and overall I think that settled a lot of issues between us."

"How so?"

"Well, I finally came to the realization that even if Fran and I couldn't be friends, she would still be an important part of my life simply because she is the mother of my children. No matter what, we will always be parents together."

"That's very true."

"So when push came to shove, I gave in to several of her requests in the final divorce settlement. I knew she was very nervous about her financial situation, so I agreed to pay an additional five years of alimony and sixty percent of our retirement funds. To be honest, I was ready to move on with my life and figured I could always earn more money. I really wanted to have a good relationship with her for the kids' sake."

"I'm really impressed, Joe. Giving Fran the extra alimony and retirement money with the realization you can always earn more is definitely a confidence-based decision. Wanting to move on with your life rather than continuing to fight over money shows you understand that time, not money, is your limiting resource."

"I guess that's true, but my main motivation was to help us both move on and allow us to share our children's joys together. I've seen other parents after a divorce being unable to be in the same room together, much less speaking to each other. I just don't want that for Mark and Marcia, and I do respect Fran as a person despite our differences."

"As I said, I'm very impressed. Now that you're divorced, are you starting to date?"

"Now that you mention it, I have been on a couple of dates since I last saw you."

"Really? Anyone I know?"

"I don't think so. One was a woman with whom I've been friends for several years. She works at another law firm in town and is also recently divorced. We talked a lot about how our divorces had affected us, but there wasn't a lot of chemistry otherwise."

"Who was your other date?"

"It was with a woman named Shirley Taylor. She is a friend of a friend. It was essentially a blind date, but we hit it off pretty well. She is really energetic, likes to travel, has tons of hobbies, and works as an interior designer."

"That sounds promising."

"I guess, but I'm not ready to rush into anything. The last thing I want right now is another long-term commitment. I need to focus on myself and the kids before I think about adding another person to the mix. Shirley and I had a very nice evening, and I imagine we will have more. But for now, that's enough for me."

"You've been through a lot of change, Joe. That's understandable."

"Let's face it. I was just a kid when Fran and I met. We were definitely in love, but we moved fast and hardly dated anyone else. I'm older and wiser now. I'm going to take this dating thing slowly and figure out what I really want."

The waiter returned with the bottle of cabernet, two fresh glasses, and salads for both men. Randy had ordered a Caesar salad, which was garnished with four neatly placed anchovies along the side. Joe's salad was a colorful medley of strawberries, pecans, and chevre on a bed of arugula. The presentation was as thoughtful as the waiter's description of the entrées, and both Randy and Joe were pleased with their choices.

Joe approved a sampling of the cabernet, and the waiter then poured each of them a glass. With a final inquiry as to any additional needs, the waiter left Randy and Joe to dine in peace.

"You haven't mentioned work yet," Randy commented in between bites of romaine. "How's the new arrangement working out?"

"It's been interesting, to say the least," Joe replied. "Overall I would say it has been positive…especially for me."

"I sense some struggles in that assessment?"

"There are definitely some struggles. Many partners have been very supportive, and a few have said the firm should have allowed this type of arrangement long ago. But some other partners are upset and want me out. They're concerned about changing the corporate culture, reducing long-term profitability, and having other partners wanting to follow my lead."

"That doesn't sound easy. How do you think it will all play out?"

"I'm not sure, and at some level I don't care that much. I would like to stay, but if I need to leave, so be it. I'm confident, with my experience and talents, that another firm will be more than happy to accommodate me."

"Look at you; another confidence-based decision," Randy said with a grin. "But how do you like the new arrangement at work?"

"I love it. I didn't expect some of the benefits it has brought me."

"Like what?"

"Well, for one, I am creating a real team within the firm. Each of us has different talents. I bring in the business, negotiate, and engage the client in strategic conversations. My partner, Phil, is a tax wizard, so he handles that part of it. Stacey Bloom has an incredible eye for detail and is a superb writer. As we have figured out each other's strong suits, we've become more efficient."

"How are the three of you getting along? Have you had many disagreements about how to handle the work or what to do for a client?"

"We've had some miscommunications, but we are figuring it out as we go. Our pattern is to defer to the partner with the most expertise in the area. If that doesn't work, we seem to go with majority rules."

"Are you more engaged at work?"

"I am. It's far from perfect, but I like spending more of my time doing what I do best. I'm happier at work than I have been in a long time."

Randy and Joe finished eating their salads, and the waiter returned to collect their plates. Every table at the restaurant was occupied, and conversations filled the room. To Joe's right, a couple held hands across a small table, sharing a thoughtful conversation together. To his left, a large family was enjoying each other's company and retelling old stories. Joe knew people came to Mickey's because of the steaks and service, but it was the atmosphere that created fond memories. And the people you're with are a big part of that atmosphere.

"So you're enjoying all this extra free time, huh?" Randy asked.

"Free time? What free time?" Joe inquired sarcastically. "I might not be working as much, but I would hardly say I have free time."

"What are you filling your schedule with now?"

"Well, it varies. With my job, I never have a consistent schedule. If we have a big deal going on, then I will still work the occasional sixty-hour week, but I'll make up the time over the next several weeks if that happens. I find myself having opportunities to take off a day or take a long weekend more often."

"I see. I guess that makes it hard to get into a groove."

"A little bit, but it's much better than before when I worked sixty hours a week or more all the time."

"I'm sure it's better. What things are you doing now that you weren't doing then?"

"Let's see. I am playing basketball and going to the gym again. You might not be able to tell, but I've actually lost fifteen pounds."

"I knew you had lost some weight, but I didn't realize it was that much. You look great."

"I feel great, and I have more energy, too."

"Feeling physically healthy is an important part of life. It's hard to be happy when you're feeling tired and run-down."

"I've also been reading a lot more, and not just business reading. I just finished a book about the Italian Renaissance. I want to be semi-knowledgeable when I go to Italy this summer."

"Weren't travel and learning two of your life priorities?"

"You've got a good memory, Randy. I still bring out that list of priorities I created with you every now and then. When I find I'm neglecting something important, I make an effort to refocus my time on what really matters."

"Joe, you get it. I know I've already said this tonight, but that's another example where you're dealing with the reality that time, not money, is your limiting resource."

"That's so true. I know I'm working twenty hours less a week on average, but that time just flies by. Even when I focus on my top ten priorities, I still feel stretched."

"I understand. Focusing your time on what matters most to you is not easy. I often say that being happy takes work. "

"Believe me, I know that's true."

"I'm sure it is. Joe, do you realize you're wealthier now than you were a year ago?"

"Here we are, having a nice conversation, and you throw out a line like that," Joe teased, smiling. "I just got divorced, lost over half my assets, and made a commitment to pay Fran alimony for a very long time. It may have been worth it, but I'm not sure I would say I'm wealthier."

"I would. I agree your financial worth has dropped, but what about your other five elements of wealth? Are you using your time better today than you were a year ago?"

"I am, and I have more free time with my new arrangement at the firm."

"Are you using your talents more effectively over the last year?"

"I am. Between the work with Wind Technologies and my new arrangement with my partners, I feel like I'm at the top of my game."

"What about your body and mind? Didn't you say you've lost weight, been working out, and are feeling great?"

"I did."

"Have you increased your wisdom?"

"You know I have."

"And your network? By reconnecting with Martin Egleston, becoming friends with Bruce Shaw, and all the people you've met through Wind Technologies, isn't it stronger?"

"It is."

"So, when you think about your money, time, talents, wisdom, body and mind, and your network combined, are you richer or poorer than you were a year ago?"

"I see your point, but I'm not going to give you the satisfaction of answering that question."

"Fair enough. I see you're still a proud man," Randy teased.

"But much less proud than I was a year ago," Joe replied.

Both Randy and Joe paused to enjoy a sip of their wine.

"Oh, by the way, I'm taking Mark and Marcia with me this summer to my family reunion in North Carolina. We haven't been in probably six or seven years."

"Are your brother and sister going to be there?"

"They are. I'm really looking forward to seeing them. We talk on the phone all the time, but I haven't actually seen them in a while."

Randy and Joe's conversation was interrupted by the smell of grilled steak as the waiter positioned each of their entrées in front of them. The waiter offered freshly ground pepper for the steaks, which both Randy and Joe accepted, and then he replenished their half-filled glasses with wine. The plates were picture-perfect, and both of them hesitated before beginning their meal. But the moment quickly passed as the aroma and their appetites overcame their admiration.

For the next few minutes, Randy and Joe ate mostly in silence, thoroughly consumed by the wonderful flavors they were tasting. Occasional comments about perfect seasoning or exquisite tenderness were the only statements made. Eventually, however, their pace slowed, and their attention returned to things more lasting.

"That steak was delicious," Joe said. "I'm all for happiness, but there's something to be said for pleasure, too."

"I can't argue with you there," Randy agreed. "Of course, that pleasure diminishes a little when the waiter brings the check."

"Good point. Why am I not surprised you would bring that up? I guess you wouldn't be a good financial advisor if you weren't thinking about finances most of the time."

"That reminds me, how is your cash flow, Joe? Between the alimony and the reduced income, I imagine you're feeling a little tight."

"I am doing okay, but I have made a few concessions."

"Like what?"

"For one, I decided to buy a more economical car that's a few years old instead of leasing a new car again. I bought a used Acura. Not only am I saving on gas, but the insurance is much less, too."

"That doesn't sound too bad."

"Fran and I also agreed to sell the house. It was too much for her anyway, and with both kids going off to college, it just made good sense."

"So that means you'll have fewer expenses?"

"Yeah. Fran will get half of the proceeds from the house as part of our agreement. With my half, I can purchase a nice home that meets my needs with only a small mortgage. I will be more than comfortable and have some extra cash for the kids' tuition and travel. I'll even be able to save a little."

"Anytime you want to revisit your projections, just let me know. But it sounds like you're pretty content with the future based on your new plan."

"I am. I think between you and Bruce at Helping Hands, I realized that I earn plenty of money to do the things that matter most to me."

The young waiter returned and cleared the table while pouring the last of the cabernet into their glasses. Joe again noticed the attention to detail as the waiter gently brushed a few fallen crumbs off the table onto a napkin.

"That was remarkable," Joe stated. "Thank you for the recommendation."

"My pleasure," the waiter replied. "May I offer you gentlemen some dessert or perhaps an after-dinner drink?"

"Randy, would you care for anything?" Joe asked.

"No, thanks. I'm content with my glass of wine," Randy said.

"I'll decline as well," Joe said. "Thank you."

The waiter left, and Joe took his glass of wine and raised it toward Randy.

"Randy, here's to a really great friend. I cannot thank you enough for helping me through all of this," Joe said.

"Thank you, Joe," Randy replied. "I know you would do the same for me."

"I certainly would...anytime. I do feel wealthy, Randy. I have enough money to be more than comfortable. I have great friends and family with whom I have deep connections. I'm using my innate talents often and feel truly engaged in life. And, for once, I feel I'm making a difference in the lives of others."

"Are you still helping Bruce at Helping Hands?"

"We communicate by email all the time and I still volunteer every couple of weeks in the office. If they need some help with project negotiations or legal advice, I'm always available for them."

"You're passionate about what they do."

"I guess I am. I've seen some pretty amazing turnarounds there among several of the mothers."

"That's really great."

"I feel like I make a difference at Helping Hands, but I know I have an effect on other people's lives, too."

"Certainly Mark and Marcia's."

"Yes, definitely. But I like to think when I do or say something of value, I inspire or influence others to do the same."

"You mean good behaviors are contagious?"

"Something like that. I think several partners at my firm are reevaluating how happy they are now that I made drastic changes in my work schedule. And I'm always amazed at how a simple compliment can make someone's day."

"I am consistently surprised at how small acts of kindness leave you feeling great. I treated a college kid to coffee at Starbucks last week, and he was so excited and grateful it made me smile the rest of the day."

The waiter returned with the check, and Joe placed his credit card in the allotted pocket. A few minutes later, the waiter collected the check and promptly returned with the charge so Joe could finalize the amount. Randy took his last sip of wine and inadvertently noticed that Joe left the young waiter a thirty-percent tip. Randy realized Joe was indeed a much happier person than he was a year ago despite all the trials and tribulations. He couldn't help but feel like the proud teacher.

"Well, I guess that's it until the next time," Joe said with a healthy grin.

"And when might that be?" Randy asked. "I don't want to go four months again."

"Me neither. How about the first Friday in June…eight o'clock at the diner?"

"Sounds great. I'll be there…as always."

THE MODEL

WEALTH AND HAPPINESS
Using Your Wealth to Create a Better Life

Why is it that so many smart, successful people find happiness so elusive despite the wealth they have accumulated? We have identified five barriers that prevent people from using their wealth to live the rich, satisfying lives they desire. Understanding those barriers and recognizing some fundamental truths about money can help you use your wealth to create the life you desire and strengthen the connection between your wealth and the happiness you seek.

Barrier #1
MISUNDERSTANDING MONEY
Defining Money As Security, Freedom, or a Way to Keep Score

Many people have a fundamental misunderstanding about the meaning of money. The purpose of wealth—indeed, the *only* purpose of wealth—is to help you create the life you desire. I have been a financial advisor for twenty-five years. In that time, I have come to realize that many people mistakenly equate money with freedom, security, or power;

those people are often afraid to spend their money. They operate under the false paradigm that every time they spend a dollar or the stock market declines, their power, freedom, or security is diminished.

Other folks use money as a way to keep score. Keeping score implies we are in a game or a race with a finish line. Imagine the finish line as the end of your life. Picture being in heaven and looking down during your funeral. The minister welcomes the crowd and lets everyone know how much the family appreciates their support. She then says that you died in the top one percent of all Americans in terms of net worth and your investment portfolio beat the S&P 500 by three points a year. She thanks everyone for coming and ends the service. How would you feel if that were your legacy? You likely would be horrified.

We want our legacy to be about how we lived our life, the relationships we created, and how we made a difference in the lives of others.

In developing the Guided Wealth Transformation® process, we uncovered some fundamental truths about money. Once these are understood, you can make progress in using your wealth to create the life you desire. Because this guide is designed to help you change course and make positive progress in your life, we identified each of these fundamental truths with the Greek letter Delta, the mathematical symbol for change.

Δ Money Is a Tool to Help You Live the Life You Desire.

Money is a tool to help you live the life you desire—nothing more, but nothing less either. You can only do four things with your money. First, you can save it or invest it in the hopes of creating a more powerful tool. Second, you can use it to help create the life you desire. Third, you can use it to enhance the lives of the people you care about. Fourth, you can use it to make a positive difference in the lives of others, creating a living legacy that represents your passions and values. When you embrace the concept that money is a tool, you can use this perspective as a filter to make sure you are not confusing money with power, freedom, or security.

Δ We Only Have Temporary Custody over Our Money.

Many of my clients were living their lives under the faulty premise that they could keep and control their wealth forever. The immutable reality is that we only have temporary custody over our money. At some point, all of us leave and our money stays behind. The goal of having money is never to die with the most. The goal is to make the best use of our money while we have control over it.

Barrier #2
IGNORING HUMAN NATURE
Believing We Are Completely Rational about Our Money

Δ Decisions about Money Are Always Emotional.

We are all human; we are all biological animals. As such, we have both an emotional and a rational part of our brain. No matter what we may tell ourselves about how rational our decisions about money are, the biological truth is that our decisions and behaviors are influenced by both our rational and emotional brains. Potential increases or decreases in our financial wealth can trigger strong emotional responses. Most people fail to recognize the true strength of the emotional part of our brain; therefore, they also fail to realize that humans often behave illogically when it comes to money. Our emotional brain can lead us to act on our anxiety, fear, and greed—and any number of other powerful emotions. Hence, if we want to use our money more effectively to build a better life for us and our loved ones, we must first acknowledge this biological imperative and then learn how to calm our fears and temper our greed so we can harness the passion and power of our emotional brain without having it overwhelm our rational brain.

Δ No Matter How Wealthy We Become, the Vast Majority of Us Suffer Anxiety over Money.

We all climb the anxiety of wealth pyramid. There are times in our lives when we get scared about losing our money. This starts as we imagine a future catastrophe, which could be anything from the market plunging to not having enough money for retirement to taking care of our aging parents. When we imagine that catastrophe, we feel fear. As our fear grows, it sets off the fight-or-flight response; blood starts to flow from our brain and gut to our major organs, arms, and legs. Our body prepares itself either to hit someone or to run away from danger. With less blood flowing to our brain, we think less clearly. We fail to see all our options and we end up feeling restricted and or even paralyzed. This biological response is what can cause the deer-in-the-headlights syndrome. When our fears become chronic, we often can feel overwhelmed and burdened, and that is never a good place to make important decisions.

Δ Confidence-Based Decisions Serve Us Better Than Fear-Based Decisions.

Consider the decisions you have made in your life. Which have served you better: fear-based or confidence-based decisions? Fear-based decisions rest on a foundation of fear; we make decisions based on what we are afraid might happen in the future. Making fear-based decisions can cause enormous damage. This damage is easy to see when it comes to investments. Those who cannot stomach scary market downturns typically lose money as they sell at market lows and buy at market highs. On the other hand, investors who are supported by faith and confidence are better able to ride out turbulent markets without making the fear-induced decision to sell. Patient, confident investors who have developed ways to keep their fears in check are more likely to enjoy long-term investment success because they have the intestinal fortitude to buy during market dips and sell when prices are high.

Confidence-based decisions can have a positive impact in many areas of our lives in part because they are more often based on reality. Decisions made from a place of confidence usually stem from a realistic assessment of our strengths and resources. When we realize the true depth of our resources and our strengths, we can feel empowered to move forward in the right direction.

How can you battle the unknown and begin to make more confidence-based decisions?

Δ Reason and Logic Are No Match for a Healthy Imagination That Fears the Worst.

Think about the last time you witnessed a three-year-old having a temper tantrum. Now imagine using logic to calm the child down. Are you smiling at the absurdity of using logic to calm a screaming child? The same holds true for adults. When we feel overwhelmed and burdened, logic is hardly ever the answer.

When we are scared, our first instinct may be to look for rational answers to calm our fears. In the story, Joe was scared about the financial impact of getting divorced and having his pay cut at work. His first instinct was to ask Randy, his financial advisor, if he was going to be okay. Joe may have been looking for a logical answer to his question, but when Randy told him he would be fine, Joe felt little relief. Logic alone could not help Joe move from fear to confidence.

Δ The Only Way to Manage Our Emotions Is with Emotional Tools.

For years, we engaged clients who were suffering from anxieties over money in rational debate, patiently explaining time and again why their worst fears were not likely to come true. If we were good at shooting down their "what-if" doomsday scenarios, anxious clients might leave the office feeling a bit better, but their fears would soon resurface with the next crisis. Despite our best efforts, rational tools simply weren't working. If you are feeling anxious, don't try to reason with your inner child. Access tools designed to help you calm down and feel more centered. Once blood begins flowing back to your oxygen-starved brain, then apply logic and reason to the situation.

Δ Accept That the Future Is Unknown and Unknowable.

As a first step, recognize we are always on the brink of the unknown, and we often fear the unknown. The truth is we can never predict the future. Although we like to imagine that our lives are safe and predictable, we constantly live on the edge of the unknown. We never know exactly what the next moment will bring. To fight our fear of the unknown, we delude ourselves into thinking we can predict the future. When things are going well, we assume that the future will be much the same as the present, and when things are going badly, we assume the worst will continue. The good news is that when we realize that we cannot predict or control the future and instead acknowledge that we always live on the edge of the unknown, we can begin to appreciate that the imagined future catastrophe we fear may not occur, and our anxiety often lessens.

Δ Faith Has the Potential to Trump Fear.

When your anxieties over wealth rise, resist the urge to engage in an unwinnable intellectual debate and use emotional exercises that can help ease your anxieties over money. One such exercise involves focusing on what you have faith in, or what you rely on, as you face an uncertain future. Some people focus on their faith in God while others focus on their faith in their spouse, family and friends, their talents, their personal character strengths like resilience, persistence, and courage, or their faith in America and Americans. Fear or doubt over a potential outcome can never be eliminated entirely with rational thought alone; only faith can bridge the divide between the known and the unknown.

What do you have faith in or what do you rely on as you face an uncertain future? How do you feel when you focus on these blessings?

Δ Gratitude Can Help Calm Our Fears.

We may view ourselves as successful, but when we compare ourselves to others who have more money (or more stuff) than we do, we often feel poorer by comparison. We can lessen the anxiety we feel by cultivating a sense of gratitude for what we have and the blessings in our lives. As we focus on all we do have instead of our material shortcomings, we can realize how fortunate we are and feel less anxious about money, more centered, and perhaps even happier.

People can be grateful for any number of things: having a great relationship with their spouse, spending time with their children, having healthy parents, enjoying good times with friends, having a job they love that puts a roof over their heads, living in America, enjoying enormous personal freedom, living at a time when technology and healthcare make a huge impact in their lives, or even having a great dog or cat to come home to. The Faith & Gratitude Exercise (see the exercises that follow) can help you rid yourself of the scarcity mentality and the anxieties that come with it.

What are you grateful for in your life? How do you feel when you focus on your blessings?

Δ Perfect Answers Don't Exist.

No financial plan or no investment strategy is ever going to provide perfect answers to every possible outcome. Do what you can to protect, preserve, and grow your wealth and learn to accept these inherent limitations on our imperfect ability to control the future. Accepting this reality can help you worry less and spend more time focusing on the things in life that bring you happiness.

Barrier #3
EQUATING MONEY WITH WEALTH

In America, a wealthy person is someone with a lot of money. The reality is that your wealth is more than money. Your wealth is about all the resources you have to create the life you desire. As we internalize this fundamental truth, we can feel less panicked during difficult economic times. Understanding the depth and breadth of all our resources often builds confidence and empowers us to create a more meaningful and satisfying life.

Δ There Are Six Components to Your Wealth.

Assessing your wealth takes a bit more work than just tallying your assets, but the results can be eye-opening. Your wealth is composed of six areas:

1. **Money:** This includes all your assets (your home, your business, your investments, bank accounts, your income from working, and all of your personal belongings). For many people, this is where the calculation of their wealth begins and ends, but money is just one resource you have to create the life you desire.

2. **Time:** Time is a unique resource. Time is the one resource that can never be renewed. If you waste time, that time is gone forever. Each of us, rich and poor alike, has the same one hundred and sixty-eight hours each week, but no one knows how many weeks we have left. For most of us, time, not money, is our limiting resource.

3. **Talents:** Each of us is blessed with our own God-given talents and talents we have spent a lifetime honing. We use those talents to earn a living, raise our children, and live our lives. Some of us have superb athletic ability. Others have a fabulous artistic sense. Still others are wonderful at working with numbers or managing people. Some of our most fulfilling times in life are when we are fully engaged in an activity that uses our Signature Talents™ to their fullest.

4. **Wisdom:** As we get older, we get wiser. We learn critical life lessons from our own experiences and from observing others. Having faced similar situations in the past, we are better equipped to seize opportunities or deal with adversity because we learned what works and what does not.

    Have you ever made a decision, such as entering into a new business or taking on a big responsibility at your church or synagogue, only to wonder why you committed to the task in the first place? In those cases, the problem is not that you lacked the necessary wisdom, but remembering to access the wisdom when you made the decision. The way to overcome that challenge is to figure out your values or pieces of wisdom for different parts of your life and to examine the list before you make critical choices. In the story, Joe's use of the Seeking Balance Worksheet to figure out which job best suited him is a good example of taking the time to access the wisdom he already possessed.

5. **Your Body and Your Mind:** We literally navigate the world using our bodies and minds. As my grandmother used to say, "If you don't have your health, you have nothing." We need sharp minds and healthy bodies to enjoy all that life has to offer. Many of us invest in our bodies and minds by eating better, exercising regularly, and staying mentally active.

6. **Your Network:** All of us are connected to a network of family, friends, colleagues, professionals, and business associates. Each person has his or her own unique talents, professional expertise, and life experiences; therefore, our personal networks are incredibly powerful. When we are facing a difficult life situation, we can learn from a friend who has dealt with a similar challenge. When we are curious how to start a new business, we may know a successful entrepreneur who can point us in the right direction. Our friends who are healthcare professionals can guide us to the right doctors or hospital when we or a family member is facing a serious illness.

Most of us underutilize our networks. Why? We underutilize our networks because of the stories we create. We are afraid of looking stupid or imposing on someone else. Yet, when we imagine the roles are reversed and someone is coming to us for advice, we typically are more than happy to help. Next time you feel stuck or need some advice, go ahead and reach out to someone in your network.

Δ In Difficult Times, Our Wealth Often Rises.

If you think of your wealth as just your financial assets, you may be poorer today than you were a few years back. If, however, you think of your wealth as including your time, talents, body and mind, wisdom, and network, you may be far richer. Ask yourself the following questions:

- Have you been forced to sharpen your talents over the past few years? Have you developed your strengths to improve your effectiveness in both your business and personal life?
- Are you making better use of your time? In business, are you spending a greater percentage of your time where you add the most value? In your personal life, are you spending more time with your most important relationships?
- Are you taking better care of your body and your mind? Are you eating better? Have you engaged in a regular exercise program?
- Have you expanded your network? Have you enhanced your relationships with the most important people in your network?
- Are you wiser today than you were a few years ago? Have you learned some important life lessons that will serve you well going forward?

When we assess our six elements of wealth instead of just counting our money, we may realize that our wealth has grown over the past few years. We are likely far richer than we ever imagined. Having a more realistic understanding of our wealth can calm our fears, increase our confidence, and empower us to dream and create a more meaningful and satisfying future.

Δ Wealth Is Synergistic.

We can enhance our ability to make an impact when we use our elements of wealth synergistically. You can give money to a nonprofit if you want to impact a community problem. If you want to magnify the impact of your gift, you can combine your time, talents, and treasure. For example, imagine the impact Joe can having on Helping Hands if he offers his financial support while helping Bruce Shaw negotiate a new lease and working with the women on finding a job that can support their family. When you use various elements of your wealth in combination, you can magnify the impact of your wealth.

Δ Focusing on Your True Wealth May Lead to Bigger and Better Answers.

By understanding your true wealth, you can appreciate that you not only have money, but you also have tools at your disposal to solve a problem or to create the life you want. Imagine having a child who recently graduated from college and has been unable to find a job. They approach you for help in paying the rent. If you equate wealth with money, your only solution is to give or loan him the rent money. If, however, you focus on your six elements of wealth, you could introduce them to influential people in your network. You might pass on some of your wisdom about how to survive on a very tight budget. You might use your talents to help them prepare for a job interview. In this case, money may help solve the immediate crisis of paying the rent, but the other tools are more important in developing a long-term solution.

When you think of your wealth as being more than just your money, you can begin to dream bigger because you think of how to use each of the six aspects of your true wealth to address a situation. By looking at all your resources, did you discover more opportunities to make a significant impact than you could if you only used money as a resource?

Barrier #4
BEING CONFUSED ABOUT WHAT MAKES YOU HAPPY

Aristotle coined this fundamental truth, "Happiness is the meaning and the purpose of life, the whole aim and end of human existence."

Aristotle may be right, but his philosophical musing begs the question: *what makes us happy?* Many of us struggle our entire lives with this question. We live in a world that bombards us with false images of happiness. Sophisticated marketers want us to believe that owning the right home, driving the right car, or taking the right luxury vacation can lead to happiness. When we buy into those messages, we quickly discover that the euphoric feeling we experience fades once we acquire those experiences or possessions. We live in a society that offers aphorisms aplenty but very little concrete guidance.

Δ Science Can Now Offer Help in Figuring Out What Makes Us Happy.

The good news is that science can offer help answering this age-old question, once exclusively the province of philosophers. While no one can tell you what will make you happy, research reveals that happiness itself is not as ephemeral or as difficult to pin down as we feared. This research indicates that there are three keys to happiness, and that happiness must be built on the foundation of a stable lifestyle.

Δ Happiness Is Built on the Foundation of a Stable Lifestyle.

It is hard to be happy if you are worried about having a safe place to sleep, putting food on the table for your loved ones, having access to quality healthcare, or having reliable transportation. Once we have enough money to securely provide for these necessities, with a little money left over for some fun, we have created the foundation we need to build upon for a happier life.

Δ The Three Keys to Happiness Are Relationships, Engagement, and Making a Positive Difference.

Happiness is all about the quality of your relationships, your ability to be fully engaged in a productive activity, and your ability to make a positive difference in the lives of others.

1. **Relationships**—Humans are highly adaptable, but we never adapt to being alone. To thrive, we all need to have close, intimate relationships based on mutual trust, mutual caring, and the ability to talk to each other without fear of judgment. Mutual trust means trusting the other person to be both honest with you and to act in your best interest. Mutual caring is sharing each other's joys and sorrows and wanting to be there when the other is going through a difficult time. Talking to each other without fear of judgment is the critical third piece. Why is this

so important? Because we self-discover as we self-disclose, and we won't self-disclose when we fear being judged.

If you want to do just one thing to become happier, focus on improving the quality of your most important relationships. You can't go to the store to buy a better relationship, but you can spend your money to create an environment to build an experience to bond with the people you love. For example, you can use your resources (time, money, body and mind) to take your family to the beach so you can give yourself an opportunity to connect (or reconnect) with them.

2. **Engagement**—Engagement is what athletes refer to as "being in the zone." We feel engaged when we are doing a high-challenge, high-skill activity that completely absorbs our attention. We are engaged when we feel like thirty minutes have passed and suddenly realize three hours have flown by. We experience this as an emotionless state that leaves us with a deep sense of satisfaction when we are finished. Furthermore, using our Signature Talents™ while being engaged often leads to both personal growth and personal achievement.

Are you fully engaged at work or at home? How often are you in the zone? If you are looking for more of those experiences, think about how you can use your Signature Talents™ more often. Joe figured out how to use his Signature Talents™ of seeing the big picture and putting the pieces together at Helping Hands to help the residents find and interview for new jobs. If you are often bored, consider how you can make a routine task more challenging. For example, give yourself a time limit to get something done while maintaining the same level of quality. Consider volunteering for a new challenge at work. When you are home, think about how to use your Signature Talents™ in a way to benefit the family. If you are particularly good at seeing possibilities, help your children think outside the box when confronted with a challenging problem.

3. **Making a Difference**—If you want to feel happier, focus on helping someone else. It doesn't have to be a life-changing event. It can be as simple as having a cup of coffee with a friend who is going through a difficult time. You can make a difference in the lives of others by engaging in a project at work that you perceive will help the world, working with a nonprofit you feel passionate about, or raising happy, well-adjusted children.

How can you make a positive impact on the lives of others? Consider calling a friend who might be struggling at home or work. Think about getting involved in a nonprofit that evokes your passions and allows you to combine your true wealth to make a real difference. Look for opportunities at work to make a difference for your colleagues, your clients or customers, or the world. Studies suggest that when you choose to do these things more often, you may be the one who benefits the most.

Δ Pleasure and Happiness Are Not the Same.

People confuse happiness with pleasure. Pleasure stems from the good feelings we experience when we stimulate our five senses. While people experience pleasure differently and from different things, pleasure can come from enjoying a luxury vacation, watching a beautiful sunset, eating the perfect New York cheesecake, or listening to a great concert. Pleasure often tends to be fleeting in nature. Think about how the exhilaration of owning a new car fades with time.

Happiness, by contrast, is built on the foundation of a stable lifestyle, and stems from the quality of our close relationships, how often we fully engage in high-challenge, high-skill activities, and making a positive difference in the lives of others. Happiness is often more enduring than pleasure. The positive energy we get from connecting with others, being engaged, or making a difference can last a long time.

Δ Pleasure Is Good; Happiness Is Great.

Please do not misunderstand: pleasure is a good thing. Having an ice-cold Coke on a hot summer day is very pleasurable and feels really good. But it is not happiness.

Pleasure is good, but happiness is great. Close relationships, being engaged in a high-challenge and high-skill activity, and making a difference in the lives of others are the cornerstones to a meaningful, happy, and satisfying life. They are the things that make life worth living, along with our faith in God, for those who have a spiritual connection.

Δ Don't Give Up Happiness for Pleasure.

Pleasure is an important part of our lives. You may enjoy having an excellent bottle of wine at a fabulous restaurant with the love of your life. However, we can quickly get in trouble when we give up happiness to buy short-term pleasures. When we stay in a high-paying job we don't enjoy so we can drive the fancy sports car, live in the big house, or vacation at a high-end resort, we likely have given up happiness to buy pleasure. When we don't pursue our passions because we are afraid of adjusting our lifestyle to fit our new budget, we may be sacrificing our happiness and filling the void with short-term pleasures.

Are you giving up happiness to purchase pleasure in any part of your life?

Barrier #5
MISMANAGING YOUR LIFE PRIORITIES:
Failing to Focus Your Wealth on What Matters Most to You

Δ The Important Often Robs Resources from the Most Important.

Most of us can separate the important things in our lives from the unimportant with relative ease, but few of us can easily distinguish what is important from what is most important. As a result, we often spend too many of our resources on the wrong things. We commit our time, talents, and treasure to things that are important to us, taking away the opportunity to spend those resources on what matters most.

The Life Priority Exercise mentioned in the story often proves both difficult and illuminating. Most people quickly realize that they have too many important priorities and they have been devoting too many resources to things that did not make their top ten list. Sometimes, the process of winnowing the list and aligning your resources with your life priorities can be heart-wrenching and slow, but, other times, you may see the disconnect and immediately redirect your resources. Figure out what your top ten life priorities are so you can devote more resources to your most important priorities.

Δ Our Most Important Priority Changes with Our Life Circumstances.

I used to have clients rank their top ten life priorities. Over time, however, I realized that ranking our priorities didn't make sense and could actually be counterproductive. The truth is that our most important priority during any given day, week, or month may change depending on our life circumstances. For example, when the big client is in town to make an important deal, work may take you away from dinner with your spouse, but when you are enjoying a family beach vacation, you may ignore even a minor emergency at work to spend time with your spouse.

Δ Life Is about Making Incremental Progress.

If you find yourself agonizing about how to align your resources to your life priorities, remember that the goal is not to achieve perfect alignment today, but to make incremental progress over time. Think of one change you can make this week and do that first. The mistake is not in making imperfect change, but in letting your anxiety and stress stop you from making any change.

Δ Understanding Your Life Priorities Can Lead to Better Life Decisions.

Many people become over-committed. We have a hard time saying no to people or causes we care about and quickly accumulate more priorities than we have time for. We end up feeling stretched to the limit and frustrated. When you identify your top life priorities, you can use your list as a filter to help decide which opportunities to pursue and which to pass on. Your filter allows you to allocate more of your resources to your most important life priorities, helps you avoid spending too much of your wealth on lesser priorities, and can help prevent you from feeling overwhelmed.

Δ Focusing on Life Priorities Can Transform a Conversation from Conflict to Cooperation.

When we work with couples, each spouse works separately to identify their top ten life priorities. This step is important because it recognizes and appreciates the reality that though we may be married, we still have our own lives, with priorities that might be uniquely ours. For example, one spouse might come from a big family and choose being connected to siblings as a top priority. The other spouse might be an only child looking to develop close friendships. Once each spouse has identified their personal top ten, we have the couple jointly decide their top life priorities as a couple and as a family.

Many couples often have disagreements over how to spend their time and money. For example, the husband might want to spend money on a family trip to the beach and the wife might want to purchase a new grill and furniture for their deck. When couples come to us with these types of disagreements, we encourage them to do two things. First, look together at all three sets of life priorities: the husband's, the wife's, and their shared life priorities. Then the couple objectively evaluates how well each option is aligned with each set of priorities. This can be challenging if the husband and wife have very different priorities. It is important they engage in a conversation about what matters most to each of them, and it is vital they look to find some common ground. Second, we urge them to try to think of alternatives that might be an even better fit than either of their initial choices. Our hope is to help them transform the conversation from who is right and who is wrong to a conversation about how to best spend their resources to create their shared vision of the future.

Understanding the five barriers is the first step on your journey from wealth to *wealth and happiness*. We hope this model, the story, and the exercises that follow help you use your wealth to create the happier and more meaningful life you desire.

EXERCISES

EXERCISE 1
Spotlight the Positives

It is a biological imperative that we are often hard-wired to pay more attention to the negatives in our lives instead of the positives. Taking time to shift our attention and focus on the positives can help us understand that life is rarely all bad or all good and can help us feel more centered, more relaxed, and better able to deal with life's inevitable problems.

Step 1: List five good things that have happened to you in the last 30 days.

Step 2: Then list why each of the five things are important to you.

Five Good Things That Have Happened To Me In The Last 30 Days	Why This Is Important To Me

You can repeat this exercise as often as you need. Try this exercise out on a friend or family member; it can help increase both the quantity and quality of your communications. This exercise can be especially helpful when you are feeling overwhelmed.

EXERCISE 2
Identify Your Top Ten Life Priorities

Most of us have far more life priorities than we have resources to fulfill them. We all have the same six elements of wealth to create the life we desire, but no matter how wealthy we may become, none of us have infinite resources. Eventually, most of us come to realize that time is often our most limiting and nonrenewable resource. When we identify our top ten life priorities and create an action plan to make progress toward fulfilling them, we typically feel happier.

Step 1: Identify your life priorities and explain why each is important. Do not rank your life priorities; simply list them, as they tend to ebb and flow rather than remain static.

What Matters Most To Me	Why This Life Priority Is Important

Step 2: Now that you have identified your top ten life priorities, you can assess whether you are spending your resources appropriately.

EXERCISE 3
Consider All Your Resources, Not Just Your Money

Many people forget that their true wealth is more than just their money. When we focus only on our money, we can create a false sense of scarcity. When faced with a problem or opportunity, it can be helpful to remember that money is just one of the six elements of wealth we have at our disposal and we need to consider all of our resources.

Step 1: Identify a specific problem or opportunity you want to address and write it below:

_____

Step 2: Identify specific ways you could use all the resources that constitute your true wealth to remedy your problem or seize upon the opportunity.

Six Elements Of True Wealth	How I Could Use This Resource To Help Me With This Problem Or Opportunity
Money	
Time	
Talents	
Body/Mind	
Wisdom	
Networks	

Step 3: Is there one idea from those listed above you could implement this week or this month? If so, list it here:

_____

You can use this rubric any time you are faced with what seems like an overwhelming problem or a complex opportunity. When you are feeling overwhelmed, keep in mind that often it is not that the problem is too big, but that you have not yet accessed all the resources you need to address it.

EXERCISE 4
Faith and Gratitude—Stepping Stones to Generating Confidence

We have the power to change how we feel by focusing on the things for which we are grateful for and identifying the things we have faith in. Try harnessing that power by trying this exercise.

Step 1: Identify at least five things that you are grateful for and at least five things you have faith in.

I Am Grateful For...	I Have Faith In...

Step 2: How do you feel when you think about the things you are grateful for and the sources of your faith?

_____

_____

Step 3: Repeat this exercise periodically whenever you feel stressed or anxious about your wealth. Try sharing this exercise with a friend or family member who may be stressed out or anxious about their wealth or a problem in their life.

EXERCISE 5
Reverse the Pleasure-for-Happiness Exchange

Pleasure is not the same as happiness. While science cannot tell you what will make you happy, research indicates that happiness comes from having good relationships, doing activities that engage you, and making a difference in the lives of others. Pleasure, on the other hand, stems from the good feelings we get from our sensory experiences and is usually short-lived.

We believe it is important not to confuse pleasure for happiness and vitally important never to exchange happiness for pleasure. Unfortunately, too many people confuse pleasure with happiness. Worse, they often make the mistake of substituting pleasure for happiness and wind up feeling unhappy and confused.

Step 1: Can you identify any areas in which you might be consistently exchanging happiness for pleasure? Can you think of ideas for how you might act differently in the future?

Sources Of Pleasure In My Life That Substitute For Happiness	What I Could Do Differently

Step 2: Is there one idea listed above that you could begin implementing this week or this month? If so, write it down here.

_____

_____

Step 3: The next time you are unsure how to proceed, consider whether you may have confused happiness and pleasure. If the proposed activity, purchase, or plan involves exchanging happiness for short-term pleasure, consider your alternatives.

EXERCISE 6
The Opportunity Filter

Being engaged is one of the three elements to true happiness. As you contemplate a potential opportunity (*e.g.*, a new job, a career change, an invitation to lead a group), it can be helpful to ask yourself if the particular opportunity reflects your life priorities, allows you to use your Signature Talents™ and has a culture that fits your work values. The right opportunity will match all three. When you find it, you'll have ample opportunities to create lots of engagement or flow experiences.

Step 1: Use the chart below to list your life priorities, Signature Talents™, and work values.

My Life Priorities	My Signature Talents ™	My Work Values

Step 2: Compare the potential opportunity with your combined list above. See where that opportunity measures up and where it may fall short. This exercise may be particularly helpful when you are comparing one opportunity to another.

EXERCISE 7
Nurture Key Relationships

Scientific research suggests that one of the three essential elements of happiness is having good relationships. The other two are doing activities that engage you and making a difference in the lives of others. If your goal is to use your wealth to make your life happier, then it makes sense to spend some of your six elements of wealth nurturing those relationships. This exercise can help you identify the key relationships in your life and develop ideas you can use to strengthen, nurture, or even repair those key relationships.

Step 1: Begin by listing five key relationships in your life.

Step 2: Next, come up with at least one step you could take to help strengthen and nurture each of the five relationships you identified in Step 1. In so doing, it may be helpful to consider each of the six elements of wealth: money, time, talents, body and mind, wisdom, and networks.

My Five Key Relationships	One Step I Could Take To Help Strengthen And Nature This Relationship

Step 3: Is there one idea listed above that you could begin implementing this week or this month? If so, write it down here.

_____

_____

EXERCISE 8
Enhance the Way You Make a Difference

Step 1: Begin by listing three key activities in which you make a difference in the lives of others. (These can be past or present activities.)

Step 2: Next, come up with at least one change you could make to make this activity even more meaningful. In so doing, it may be helpful to consider how you might use each of the six elements of wealth: money, time, talents, body and mind, wisdom, and networks.

Three Key Activities In Which I Make A Difference	One Change I Could Make That Could Make This Activity Even More Meaningful

Step 3: Is there one idea listed above that you could begin implementing this week or this month? If so, write it down here.

_____

_____

REFERENCES

I n his boundless quest to imagine, create, perfect, and continually evolve the **Guided Wealth Transformation**® model, the author read and relied upon a wide variety of works from many gifted researchers, psychologists, philosophers, writers, and fellow visionaries who are likewise engaged in the noble and never-ending search for truth and happiness. David gratefully acknowledges the tremendous work underlying these excellent books and articles, and apologizes for any misunderstandings or inadvertent misrepresentations of their hypotheses or conclusions. Any errors contained herein are the author's alone and are not the responsibility of these authors.

For those who are interested in doing additional reading on the fascinating and sometimes confounding topics of happiness, human psychology, and the psychology of investing, David is pleased to recommend these books for further exploration. Happy reading!

- Achor, Shawn, *The Happiness Advantage: The Seven Principles of Positive Psychology That Fuel Success and Performance at Work* (2010)
- Akerlof, George A., and Shiller, Robert J., *Animal Spirits: How Human Psychology Drives the Economy, and Why It Matters for Global Capitalism* (2009)
- Dalai Lama, *The Art of Happiness, 10th Anniversary Edition: A Handbook for Living* (2009)
- Ariely, Dan, *Predictably Irrational, Revised and Expanded Edition: The Hidden Forces That Shape Our Decisions* (2009)
- Ben-Shahar, Tal, Ph.D., *The Pursuit of Perfect: How to Stop Chasing Perfection and Start Living a Richer, Happier Life* (2009)
- Brooks, David, *The Social Animal: The Hidden Sources of Love, Character, and Achievement* (2011)
- Buckingham, Marcus, and Coffman, Curt, *First, Break All the Rules: What the World's Greatest Managers Do Differently* (1999)
- Chapman, Gary D., *The 5 Love Languages: The Secret to Love That Lasts* (2010)
- Colvin, Geoff, *Talent Is Overrated: What Really Separates World-Class Performers from Everybody Else* (2008)
- Corbett, David D., *Portfolio Life: The New Path to Work, Purpose, and Passion After 50* (2006)
- Csikszentmihalyi, Mihaly, *Finding Flow: The Psychology of Engagement with Everyday Life* (1998)
- Ferrazzi, Keith, *Who's Got Your Back: The Breakthrough Program to Build Deep, Trusting Relationships That Create Success—and Won't Let You Fail* (2009)
- Frederickson, Barbara, *Positivity: Groundbreaking Research Reveals How to Embrace the Hidden Strength of Positive Emotions, Overcome Negativity, and Thrive* (2009)

- Gilbert, Daniel, *Stumbling on Happiness* (2006)
- Gottman, John, *The Seven Principles for Making Marriage Work* (1999)
- Haidt, Jonathan, *The Happiness Hypothesis: Finding Modern Truth in Ancient Wisdom* (2005)
- Hanson, Rick (author), and Mendius, Richard (collaborator), *Buddha's Brain: The Practical Neuroscience of Happiness, Love, and Wisdom* (2009)
- Hirsch, Sherre, *We Plan, God Laughs: What to Do When Life Hits You Over the Head* (2008)
- Johnson, Sue, *Hold Me Tight: Seven Conversations for a Lifetime of Love* (2008)
- Kushner, Harold S., *Conquering Fear: Living Boldly in an Uncertain World* (2009)
- Kushner, Harold S., *Living a Life That Matters* (2000)
- Kushner, Harold S., *Overcoming Life's Disappointments* (2006)
- Kinder, George, *The Seven Stages of Money Maturity: Understanding the Spirit and Value of Money in Your Life* (1999)
- Lyubormirsky, Sonja, *The How of Happiness: A New Approach to Getting the Life You Want* (2008)
- Patterson, Kerry, Grenny, Joseph, McMillan, Ron, and Switzler, Al, *Crucial Conversations: Tools for Talking When Stakes Are High* (2002)
- Prager, Dennis, *Happiness Is a Serious Problem: A Human Nature Repair Manual* (1998)
- Roa, Srikumar S., *Happiness at Work: Be Resilient, Motivated, and Successful—No Matter What* (2010)
- Richard, Matthieu, *Happiness: A Guide to Developing Life's Most Important Skill* (2006)
- Seligman, Ph.D., Martin E.P., *Authentic Happiness: Using the New Positive Psychology to Realize Your Potential for Lasting Fulfillment* (2002)

- Seligman, Ph.D., Martin E.P., *Flourish: A Visionary New Understanding of Happiness and Well-Being* (2011)
- Shapiro, Rabbi Rami M., *The Sacred Art of Lovingkindness: Preparing to Practice* (2006)
- Tolle, Eckhardt, *A New Earth: Awakening to Your Life's Purpose* (2005)
- Tolle, Eckhardt, *The Power of Now: A Guide to Spiritual Enlightenment* (1999)
- Zweig, Jason, *Your Money and Your Brain: How the New Science of Neuroeconomics Can Help Make You Rich* (2007)

A FINAL NOTE
About Wealth and Happiness and the GWT® Exercises

Remember, the goal of these exercises is not to achieve immediate and perfect alignment between your life priorities and Signature Talents™ or to use all of your resources perfectly from this point forward. We each pursue happiness in our own way and at our own pace. Change is not always easy—especially change that involves shedding our old paradigms about money, wealth, and happiness—but I believe that the privilege of helping people come to new understandings about their wealth and happiness so they can better use their wealth to create the lives they desire is my highest and best life's purpose. For additional resources and help, please visit our website, www.gvfinancial.com, or email us at info@gvfinancial.com. May your wealth always be abundant and may you find happiness in life's journey.

—David Geller

IMPORTANT DISCLAIMERS, DISCLOSURES, AND TERMS OF USE

The information provided herein is for general educational and entertainment purposes only and should not be considered an individualized recommendation or personalized investment or financial advice, nor should the information provided herein be considered legal, tax, accounting, counseling, or therapeutic advice of any kind. The material herein includes opinions of the author, is subject to change without notice, and may not reflect the views of GV Financial Advisors, Inc., as a whole. This material is not intended to be relied upon as a forecast, research, or investment advice regarding a particular investment or the markets in general, nor is it intended to predict or depict performance of any investment or personal strategy. Always consult a financial advisor to determine what investment strategy might be best for you and consult other professionals as appropriate. The material is not intended to provide personal investment advice and it does not take into account the specific investment objectives, financial situation, and the particular needs of any specific person. Any examples or characters mentioned herein are hypothetical in nature, purely fictitious, and do not reflect any actual persons living or dead. GV Financial Advisors, together with its affiliated companies, directors, officers, and employees, make no representations, whether express or implied, as to any expected outcome based on the use of any of the information or exercises presented herein. Users assume all responsibilities for the use of these materials. Neither GV Financial Advisors nor its affiliated companies nor any director, officer, or employee of GV Financial Advisors or its affiliated companies accepts any liability whatsoever for any direct, indirect, or consequential damages or losses arising from any use of this document or its contents. Please refer to additional terms of use and disclaimers on our website at: http://www.gvfinancial.com.

GVFA 2012 0003 DOFU 1/2012